The Pocket Guide to TCP/IP Sockets

C Version

The Morgan Kaufmann Series in Networking
Series Editor: David Clark, M.I.T.

The Pocket Guide to TCP/IP Sockets: C Version
Michael J. Donahoo and Kenneth L. Calvert

Multicast Communication: Protocols, Programming, and Applications
Ralph Wittmann and Martina Zitterbart

MPLS: Technology and Applications
Bruce Davie and Yakov Rekhter

High-Performance Communication Networks, 2e
Jean Walrand and Pravin Varaiya

Computer Networks: A Systems Approach, 2e
Larry L. Peterson and Bruce S. Davie

Internetworking Multimedia
Jon Crowcroft, Mark Handley, and Ian Wakeman

Understanding Networked Applications: A First Course
David G. Messerschmitt

Integrated Management of Networked Systems: Concepts, Architectures, and their Operational Application
Heinz-Gerd Hegering, Sebastian Abeck, and Bernhard Neumair

Virtual Private Networks: Making the Right Connection
Dennis Fowler

Networked Applications: A Guide to the New Computing Infrastructure
David G. Messerschmitt

Modern Cable Television Technology: Video, Voice, and Data Communications
Walter Ciciora, James Farmer, and David Large

Switching in IP Networks: IP Switching, Tag Switching, and Related Technologies
Bruce S. Davie, Paul Doolan, and Yakov Rekhter

Wide Area Network Design: Concepts and Tools for Optimization
Robert S. Cahn

Optical Networks: A Practical Perspective
Rajiv Ramaswami and Kumar Sivarajan

Practical Computer Network Analysis and Design
James D. McCabe

Frame Relay Applications: Business and Technology Case Studies
James P. Cavanagh

For further information on these books and for a list of forthcoming titles, please visit our Web site at *www.mkp.com.*

The Pocket Guide to TCP/IP Sockets

C Version

Michael J. Donahoo

Baylor University

Kenneth L. Calvert

University of Kentucky

MORGAN KAUFMANN PUBLISHERS

AN IMPRINT OF ACADEMIC PRESS

A Harcourt Science and Technology Company

SAN FRANCISCO   SAN DIEGO   NEW YORK   BOSTON
LONDON   SYDNEY   TOKYO

Senior Editor   Jennifer Mann
Senior Production Editor   Cheri Palmer
Editorial Coordinator   Karyn Johnson
Cover Design   Ross Carron Design
Text Design   Side by Side Studios
Composition/Illustration   Windfall Software, using ZzTeX
Copyeditor   Erin Milnes
Proofreader   Jennifer McClain
Indexer   Ty Koontz
Printer   Courier Corporation

Designations used by companies to distinguish their products are often claimed as trademarks or registered trademarks. In all instances where Morgan Kaufmann Publishers is aware of a claim, the product names appear in initial capital or all capital letters. Readers, however, should contact the appropriate companies for more complete information regarding trademarks and registration.

ACADEMIC PRESS
A Harcourt Science and Technology Company
525 B Street, Suite 1900, San Diego, CA 92101-4495, USA
http://www.academicpress.com

Academic Press
Harcourt Place, 32 Jamestown Road, London, NW1 7BY, United Kingdom
http://www.academicpress.com

Morgan Kaufmann Publishers
340 Pine Street, Sixth Floor, San Francisco, CA 94104-3205, USA
http://www.mkp.com

Library of Congress Cataloging-in-Publication Data

Donahoo, Michael J.
   The pocket guide to TCP/IP sockets : C version / Michael J. Donahoo, Kenneth L. Calvert.
      p.   cm.
   ISBN 1-55860-686-6
   1. Application program interfaces (Computer software)   2. TCP/IP (Computer network protocol)   3. C (Computer program language)   I. Calvert, Kenneth L.   II. Title.
   QA76.76.A63 D66 2001
   005.7′13762—dc21   00-055020

This book is printed on acid-free paper.

Contents

Preface   ix

PART 1 Tutorial   1

1 Introduction   3
   1.1   Networks, Packets, and Protocols   3
   1.2   About Addresses   5
   1.3   Clients and Servers   6
   1.4   What Is a Socket?   7
          Thought Questions   8

2 Basic Sockets   9
   2.1   Creating and Destroying   9
   2.2   Specifying Addresses   10
   2.3   TCP Client   12
   2.4   TCP Server   17
          Thought Questions   23

3 Constructing Messages   25
   3.1   Encoding Data   26
   3.2   Byte Ordering   28
   3.3   Alignment and Padding   30
   3.4   Framing and Parsing   31
          Thought Questions   33

4   **Using UDP Sockets   35**
4.1   UDP Client   36
4.2   UDP Server   39
4.3   Sending and Receiving with UDP Sockets   41
        Thought Questions   42

5   **Socket Programming   43**
5.1   Socket Options   43
5.2   Signals   44
5.3   Nonblocking I/O   50
5.4   Multitasking   60
5.5   Multiplexing   72
5.6   Multiple Recipients   77
        Thought Questions   85

6   **Under the Hood   87**
6.1   Buffering and TCP   89
6.2   Deadlock   91
6.3   Performance Implications   92
6.4   TCP Socket Life Cycle   93
6.5   Demultiplexing Demystified   100
        Thought Questions   102

7   **Domain Name Service   103**
7.1   Mapping Between Names and Internet Addresses   104
7.2   Finding Service Information by Name   106

PART 2   API Reference   109

API Reference   111

    Data Structures   111
        sockaddr   111
        sockaddr_in   111

    Socket Setup   112
        socket()   112
        bind()   112
        getsockname()   113

Socket Connection 113
  connect() 113
  listen() 114
  accept() 114
  getpeername() 114

Socket Communication 115
  send() 115
  sendto() 115
  recv() 116
  recvfrom() 116
  close() 117
  shutdown() 117

Socket Control 118
  getsockopt() 118
  setsockopt() 118

Binary/String Conversion 119
  inet_ntoa() 119
  inet_addr() 119
  htons(), htonl(), ntohs(), ntohl() 119

Host and Service Information 120
  gethostname() 120
  gethostbyname() 120
  gethostbyaddr() 121
  getservbyname() 121
  getservbyport() 122

Bibliography 123

Index 125

Preface

For years, college courses in computer networking were taught with little or no "hands on" experience. For various reasons, including some good ones, instructors approached the principles of computer networking primarily through equations, analyses, and abstract descriptions of protocol stacks. Textbooks might include code, but it was unconnected to anything students could get their hands on. Perhaps in an ideal world this would suffice, but we believe that students learn better when they can see (and then build) concrete examples of the principles at work. Fortunately, such examples abound today. The Internet has become a part of everyday life, and access to its services is readily available to most students (and their programs).

The *Berkeley Sockets interface*, known universally as "sockets" for short, is the de facto standard application programming interface (API) for networking, spanning a wide range of operating systems. The sockets API was designed to provide *generic* access to interprocess communication services that might be implemented by whatever protocols were supported on a particular platform—IPX, Appletalk, TCP/IP, and so on. As a consequence of this generic approach the sockets API may appear dauntingly complicated at first. But, in fact, the basics of network programming using the Internet (TCP/IP) protocols are not difficult. The sockets interface has been around for a long time—at least in "Internet time"—but it is likely to remain important for the foreseeable future.

We wrote this book to improve the support for socket-based programming exercises in our own networking courses. Although some networking texts deal with network programming, we know of none that cover TCP/IP sockets. Excellent reference books on TCP/IP socket programming exist, but they are too large and comprehensive to be considered as a supplement to a networking text. UNIX "man pages" are okay for reference but do not make a very good tutorial. Our goal, therefore, was to provide a gentle introduction, and a handy reference, that would allow students to dive right in without too much handholding.

Enabling students to get their hands on real network services via the sockets interface has several benefits. First, for a surprising number of people, socket programming is the first exposure to concrete realizations of concepts previously seen only in the abstract. Dealing with the very real consequences of messy details, such as the layout of data structures in memory, seems to trigger a kind of epiphany in some students, and this experience has consequences far beyond the networking course. Second, we find that students who understand how application programs *use* the services of TCP/IP generally have an easier time grasping the principles of the underlying protocols that *implement* those services. Finally, basic socket programming skills are a springboard to more advanced assignments, which support learning about routing algorithms, multimedia protocols, medium access control, and so on.

Intended Audience

This book is aimed primarily at students in introductory courses in computer networks, either upper-level undergraduate or graduate. It is intended as a supplement, to be used with a traditional textbook, which should explain the problems and principles of computer networks. At the same time, we have tried to make the book reasonably self-contained (except for the assumed background) so that it can also be used, for example, in courses on operating systems or distributed computing. We have purposely limited coverage in order to keep the price low enough to be reasonable as a supplementary text for such a course. An additional target audience consists of practitioners who know some C and want to learn sockets. This book should take you far enough so that you can start experimenting and learning on your own.

We assume basic programming skills and experience with C and UNIX. You are expected to be conversant with C concepts such as pointer manipulation and type casting and should have a basic understanding of how data structures are implemented in memory, including the binary representation of data. Some of our examples are factored into files that should be compiled separately; we assume that you can deal with that.

Here is a little test: If you can puzzle out what the following code fragment does, you should have no problem with the code in this book:

```c
typedef struct {
  int a;
  short s[2];
} MSG;

MSG *mp, m = {4, 1, 0};
char  *fp, *tp;
mp = (MSG *) malloc(sizeof(MSG));
for (fp = (char *)&m.s, tp = (char *)mp->s; tp < (char *)(mp+1);)
  *tp++ = *fp++;
```

If you do not understand this fragment, do not despair (there is nothing quite so convoluted in our code), but you might want to refer to your favorite C programming book to find out what is going on here.

You should also be familiar with the UNIX notions of process/address space, command-line arguments, program termination, and regular file input and output. The material in Chapters 4 and 5 assumes a somewhat more advanced grasp of UNIX. Some exposure to networking concepts such as protocols, addresses, clients, and servers will be helpful.

Platform Requirements

You are assumed to have access to a computer equipped with an operating system and C compiler that support the sockets interface, as well as a connection to the Internet or a private network running TCP/IP. Our presentation is UNIX-based. When we were developing this book, several people urged us to include code for Windows as well as UNIX. It was not possible to do so for various reasons including the target length (and price) we set for the book.

For those who only have access to Windows platforms, please note that the examples in Chapters 1–3 require minimal modifications to work with WinSock. You have to change the include files and add a setup call at the beginning of the program and a cleanup call at the end. Most of the other examples require very slight additional modifications. A few, however, are so dependent on the UNIX programming model that it does not make sense to port them to WinSock. WinSock-ready versions of the other examples, as well as detailed descriptions of the code modifications required, are available from the book's Web site at *www.mkp.com/socket*. Note also that almost all of our example code works with minimal modifications under the Cygwin portability package for Windows, which is available (at the time of this writing) from Red Hat Software. See the Web site for details.

Portability and Coding Styles

The example programs included here have all been tested (and should compile and run without modification) on both Linux and Solaris. We have tried to make the code as portable as possible and conform to the POSIX standard wherever possible without compromising portability. Unfortunately, these goals sometimes conflict. For example, gcc under Solaris wants the sixth argument of recvfrom() to be a signed **int**, whereas under Linux it wants **unsigned int**. POSIX says it should be a **socklen_t**, which is actually **uint32_t**. We have used **unsigned int**. (Because the POSIX types (e.g., **int8_t**) are not universally supported, we are not using them in this text.)

Header (.h) file locations and dependencies are, alas, far from standard and may require some fiddling on your system. Socket option support also varies widely across systems; we have tried to focus on those that are most universally supported. Consult your API documentation for system specifics.

The two authors' coding styles turned out to be rather different; what you see here is a compromise that we both could live with. Please be aware that although we strive for robustness, the primary goal of our code examples is pedagogy, and the code is not necessarily production quality. Especially in the early examples, we have sacrificed some robustness for brevity and clarity.

Approach

This book will not make you an expert! That takes years of experience, as well as other, more comprehensive sources [4, 16]. However, we hope it will be useful as a resource, even to those who already know quite a bit about sockets. (Each of us learned some things in writing it.)

The first part of the book is a tutorial, which begins with "just enough" of the big picture, then quickly gets into code basics via some example programs. The first four chapters aim to get you quickly to the point of constructing simple clients and servers, such as might be needed to complete introductory assignments. After that we branch out in Chapter 5, introducing some of the many different ways to use sockets. Chapter 6 returns to basic socket operation to provide more in-depth coverage of some of the underlying mechanisms and some pitfalls to watch out for. Chapter 7 describes domain names and how they can be used to obtain Internet addresses.

Chapters 5, 6, and 7 are essentially independent and may be presented in any order. Also, if you are familiar with socket basics, you may wish to skip the introductory material and go directly to those chapters. We placed the material on names at the very end of the tutorial part in order to emphasize that the TCP/IP and UDP/IP services are completely independent of the domain name system—a convenience, rather than an integral part of the network service.

Part II is a reference section that provides the declaration and a description of the parameters for the main functions that make up the sockets API. It is intended to serve as a quick reference for both novices and more advanced network programmers.

Acknowledgments

We would like to thank all the people who helped make this book a reality. Despite the book's brevity, many hours went into reviewing the original proposal and the draft, and the reviewers' input has significantly shaped the final result.

First, thanks to those who meticulously reviewed the draft of the text and made suggestions for improvement. These include (in alphabetical order) Michel Barbeau, Carleton University; Steve Bernier, Communications Research Center; Arian Durresi, Ohio State University; Gary Harkin, University of Montana; Ted Herman, University of Iowa; Lee Hollaar, University of Utah; Shunge Li, GTE; Willis Marti, Texas A&M; Kihong Park, Purdue University; Dan Schmitt, Texas A&M; and CSI4321, Spring 2000. Paul Linton of the University of Kentucky helped in testing the code for portability. Any errors that remain are, of course, our responsibility. We are very interested in weeding out such errors in future printings, so if you find one, please send email to either of us. We will maintain an errata list on the book's Web page.

Thanks are also due to those who reviewed the original proposal and thereby helped us decide what to put in and what to leave out. Those not already mentioned include (again, in alphabetical order): David Hutchison, Lancaster University; Ivan Marsic, Rutgers University; Michael Scott, University of Rochester; Robert Strader, Stephen F. Austin State University; Ben Wah, University of Illinois-Urbana; and Ellen Zegura, Georgia Tech.

Finally, we are grateful to the folks at Morgan Kaufmann. They take a hands-on approach to development that contributes significantly to the ultimate text quality. Jennifer Mann, our editor, and Karyn Johnson, editorial assistant, have worked hard to provide invaluable guidance throughout this process. We are also grateful to Cheri Palmer, our production editor, who has been very willing to work with us on the design and "look and feel" of the text; we hope you like the result.

Feedback

We invite your suggestions for improvement of any aspect of this book. You can send feedback via the book's Web page, which is maintained by the publisher, or you can send us email to the addresses below.

M.J.D.   jeff_donahoo@baylor.edu

K.L.C.   calvert@dcs.uky.edu

PART 1

TUTORIAL

chapter **1**

Introduction

Millions of computers all over the world are now connected to the worldwide network known as the Internet. The Internet enables programs running in computers thousands of miles apart to communicate and exchange information. If you have a computer connected to a network, you may have used a Web browser—a typical program that makes use of the Internet. What does such a program do to communicate with others over a network? The answer varies with the application and the operating system, but a great many programs get access to network communication services through the "sockets" programming interface. The goal of this book is to get you started writing programs that use the sockets API.

Before delving into the details of the API, it is worth taking a brief look at the big picture of networks and protocols to see how an application programming interface for TCP/IP fits in. Our goal here is *not* to teach you how networks and TCP/IP work—many fine texts are available for that purpose [2, 4, 10, 15, 20]—but rather to introduce some basic concepts and terminology.

1.1 Networks, Packets, and Protocols

A computer network consists of machines interconnected by communication channels. We call these machines *hosts* and *routers*. Hosts are computers that run applications such as your Web browser; the application programs running in hosts are really the "users" of the network. Routers are machines whose job is to relay or *forward* information from one communication channel to another. They may run programs but typically do not run application programs. For our purposes, a *communication channel* is a means of conveying sequences of bytes from one host to another; it may be a broadcast technology like Ethernet, a dial-up modem connection, or something more sophisticated.

Routers are important simply because it is not practical to connect every host directly to every other host. Instead, a few hosts connect to a router, which connects to other routers, and so on to form the network. This arrangement lets each machine get by with a relatively

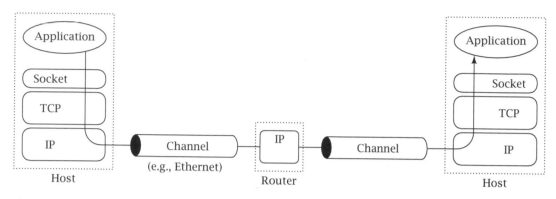

Figure 1.1: A TCP/IP network.

small number of communication channels; most hosts need only one. Programs that exchange information over the network, however, do not interact directly with routers and generally remain blissfully unaware of their existence.

By "information" here we mean sequences of *bytes* that are constructed and interpreted by programs; we will see examples later. In the context of computer networks these byte sequences are generally called *packets*. A packet contains control information that the network uses to do its job and sometimes also includes user data. An example is information about the packet's destination. Routers use such control information to figure out how to forward each packet.

A *protocol* is an agreement about the packets exchanged by communicating programs and what they mean. A protocol tells how packets are structured—for example, where the destination information is located in the packet and how big it is—as well as how the information is to be interpreted. A protocol is usually designed to solve a specific problem using given capabilities. For example, the Hypertext Transfer Protocol (HTTP) solves the problem of transferring hypertext objects between servers where they are stored and Web browsers that make them available to humans.

Implementing a useful network requires that a large number of different problems be solved. To keep things manageable and modular, different protocols are designed to solve different sets of problems. TCP/IP is one such collection of solutions, sometimes called a *protocol suite* or *protocol family*. It happens to be the protocol family used in the "capital-I Internet," but it can be used in stand-alone private networks as well; henceforth when we say "the network," we mean any network that uses the TCP/IP protocol family. The main protocols in the TCP/IP family are the Internet Protocol (IP), the Transmission Control Protocol (TCP), and the User Datagram Protocol (UDP).

It turns out to be useful to organize protocols in a family into *layers*; TCP/IP and virtually all other protocol families are organized this way. Figure 1.1 shows the relationships among the protocols, applications, and the sockets API in the hosts and routers, as well as the flow of data from one application to another. The boxes labeled TCP and IP represent implementations of those protocols. Such implementations typically reside in the operating system of a host. Applications access the services provided by UDP and TCP through the sockets API. The arrow depicts the flow of data from the application, through the TCP and IP implementations, through the network, and back up through the IP and TCP implementations at the other end.

In TCP/IP, the bottom layer consists of the underlying communication channels, for example, Ethernet or dial-up modem connections. Those channels are used by the *network layer*, which deals with the problem of forwarding packets toward their destination (i.e., what routers do). The single network layer protocol in the TCP/IP family is the Internet Protocol; it solves the problem of making the sequence of channels and routers between any two hosts look like a single host-to-host channel.

The Internet Protocol provides a *datagram* service: Every packet is handled and delivered by the network independently, like telegrams or parcels sent via the postal system. To make this work, each IP packet has to contain the *address* of its destination, just as every package you mail is addressed to somebody. (We'll say more about addresses shortly.) Although most parcel delivery companies guarantee delivery of a package, IP is only a best-effort protocol: It attempts to deliver each packet, but it can (and occasionally does) lose, reorder, or duplicate packets in transit through the network.

The layer above IP is called the *transport layer.* It offers a choice between two protocols: TCP and UDP. Each builds on the service provided by IP, but they do so in different ways to provide different kinds of channels, which are used by *application protocols* with different needs.

TCP and UDP have one function in common: addressing. Recall that IP delivers packets to hosts; clearly, a finer granularity of addressing is needed to get a packet to a particular application, perhaps one of many using the network in the same host. Both TCP and UDP use addresses called *port numbers* so that applications within hosts can be identified. They are called *end-to-end transport* protocols because they carry data all the way from one program to another (whereas IP carries data from one host to another).

TCP is designed to detect and recover from the losses, duplications, and other errors that may occur in the host-to-host channel provided by IP. TCP provides a *reliable byte-stream* channel, so that applications don't have to deal with these problems. Using TCP is similar to file I/O, though there are important differences. UDP, on the other hand, does not attempt to recover from losses and reorderings; it simply extends the IP best-effort datagram service so that it works between applications instead of between hosts. Thus, applications that use UDP must be prepared to deal with losses, duplication, and so on.

1.2 About Addresses

Before a program can communicate with another program, it must tell the network "where" to find the other program—similar to when you send a letter, you provide the address of the recipient of a letter in a form that the postal service can understand, and the way that you give the telephone system the number of the telephone you are calling. In TCP/IP, it takes two pieces of information to identify a particular program: an *Internet address*, used by IP, and a *port number*, the additional address interpreted by the transport protocol (TCP or UDP).

Internet addresses are 32-bit binary numbers.[1] In writing down Internet addresses for human consumption (as opposed to using them inside applications), we typically show them as a string of four decimal numbers separated by periods (e.g., "10.1.2.3"); this is called the "dotted-quad" notation. The four numbers in a dotted-quad string represent the contents of the four bytes of the Internet address, thus each is a number between 0 and 255.

Technically, each Internet address refers to the connection between a host and an underlying communication channel, such as a dial-up modem or Ethernet card. Because each such network connection belongs to a single host, an Internet address identifies a host as well as its connection to the network. However, because a host can have multiple physical connections to the network, one host can have multiple Internet addresses.

Most likely you are accustomed to referring to hosts by *name* (e.g., "host.example.com"). However, the Internet protocols deal with numerical addresses, not names. Services exist that can map names to Internet addresses (see Chapter 7). Since names are just a level of indirection on top of the Internet protocols, we will stick with using Internet addresses in our programming examples until later in the book.

The port number in TCP or UDP is always interpreted relative to an Internet address. Returning to our earlier analogies, a port number corresponds to a room number at a given street address, say, that of a large building. The postal service uses the street address to get the letter to a mailbox; whoever empties the mailbox is then responsible for getting the letter to the proper room within the building. Or consider a company with an internal telephone system: To speak to an individual in the company, you first dial the company's main number to connect to the internal telephone system and then dial the extension of the particular telephone of the individual you wish to speak with. In these analogies, the Internet address is the street address or the company's main number, whereas the port corresponds to the room number or telephone extension. Port numbers are 16-bit unsigned binary numbers, so each one is in the range 1 to 65,535 (0 is reserved).

1.3 Clients and Servers

In our postal and telephone analogies, each communication is initiated by one party, who sends a letter or dials the telephone call, while the other party responds to the initiator's contact by sending a return letter or picking up the phone and talking. Internet communication is again similar. The terms *client* and *server* refer to these roles: The client program initiates

---

[1] Throughout this book the term *Internet address* refers to the addresses used with the current version of IP, which is version 4 [11]. Because it is expected that a 32-bit address space will be inadequate for future needs, a new version of IP has been defined [5]; it provides the same service but has much bigger Internet addresses (128 bits). "IPv6," as the new version is known, has not been widely deployed; the sockets API will require some changes to deal with its much larger addresses [6].

communication, while the server program waits passively for and then responds to clients that contact it. Together, the client and server compose the *application*. The terms "client" and "server" are descriptive of the typical situation in which the server makes a particular capability—for example, a database service—available to any client that is able to communicate with it using the TCP/IP protocols.

Whether a program is acting as a client or server determines the general form of its use of the sockets API to communicate with its *peer*. (The client is the peer of the server and vice versa.) Beyond that, the client-server distinction is important because *the client needs to know the server's address and port initially*, but not vice versa. With the sockets API, the server can, if necessary, learn the client's address information when it receives the initial communication from the client. This is analogous to a telephone call—the callee in general does not need to know the telephone number of the caller.

How does a client find out a server's IP address and port number? Usually, the client knows the name of the server it wants, for example, from a Universal Resource Locator (URL) such as "http://www.mkp.com," and uses the name resolution service (see Chapter 7) to learn the corresponding Internet address.

Finding a server's port number is a different story. In principle, servers can use any port, but the client must be able to learn what it is. In the Internet, there is a convention of assigning *well-known port numbers* to certain applications. The Internet Assigned Number Authority (IANA) oversees this assignment. For example, port number 21 has been assigned to the File Transfer Protocol. When you run an FTP client application, it tries to contact the FTP server on that port by default. A list of all the assigned port numbers is maintained by the numbering authority of the Internet (see http://www.isi.edu/in-notes/iana/assignments/port-numbers).

1.4 What Is a Socket?

A socket is an abstraction through which an application may send and receive data, in much the same way as an open file allows an application to read and write data to stable storage. A socket allows an application to "plug in" to the network and communicate with other applications that are also plugged in to the same network. Information written to the socket by an application on one machine can be read by an application on a different machine, and vice versa.

Sockets come in different flavors, corresponding to different underlying protocol families and different stacks of protocols within a family. In this book we deal only with the TCP/IP protocol family. The main flavors of sockets in the TCP/IP family are *stream* sockets and *datagram* sockets. Stream sockets use TCP as the end-to-end protocol (with IP underneath) and thus provide a reliable byte-stream service. Datagram sockets use UDP (again, with IP underneath) and thus provide a best-effort datagram service that applications can use to send individual messages up to about 65,500 bytes in length. Stream and datagram sockets are also supported by other protocol suites; however, in this book we deal only with TCP stream sockets and UDP datagram sockets.

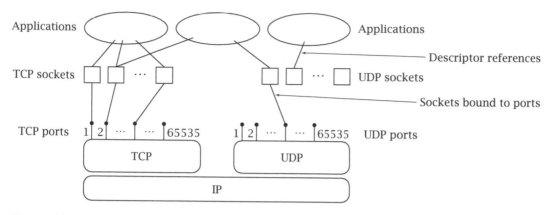

Figure 1.2: Sockets, protocols, and ports.

A socket using the TCP/IP protocol family is uniquely identified by an Internet address, an end-to-end protocol (TCP or UDP), and a port number. When a socket is first created, it has an associated protocol but no Internet address or port number. Until a socket is *bound* to a port number, it cannot receive messages from a remote application. As we proceed, we will encounter several ways for a socket to become bound to an address.

Figure 1.2 depicts the logical relationships among applications, socket abstractions, protocols, and port numbers within a single host. Note that a single socket abstraction can be referenced by multiple application programs. Each program that has a reference (called a *descriptor*) to a particular socket can communicate through that socket. Earlier we said that a port identifies an application on a host. Actually, a port identifies a socket on a host. From Figure 1.2, we see that multiple programs on a host can access the same socket. In practice, separate programs that access the same socket would usually belong to the same application (e.g., multiple copies of a Web server program), although in principle they could belong to different applications.

Thought Questions

1. Can you think of a real-life example of communication that does not fit the client-server model?

2. To how many different kinds of "network" is your home connected? How many support two-way communication?

chapter **2**

Basic Sockets

We are now ready to begin using the sockets API. Although clients and servers differ in some aspects of their use of the API, other aspects are common across clients and servers and across TCP and UDP sockets. After dealing with these common aspects, we present the details through an example client and server.

2.1 Creating and Destroying

To communicate using TCP or UDP, a program begins by asking the operating system to create an instance of the socket abstraction. The function that accomplishes this is socket(); its parameters specify the flavor of socket needed by the program.

---

int socket(**int** *protocolFamily*, **int** *type*, **int** *protocol*)

The first parameter determines the *protocol family* of the socket. Recall that the sockets API provides a generic interface for a large number of protocol families. The constant PF_INET specifies a socket that uses protocols from the Internet protocol family. Since this text does not deal with any other protocol families, we will always supply PF_INET for the protocol family.

The second parameter specifies the *type* of the socket. The type determines the semantics of data transmission with the socket—for example, whether transmission is reliable, whether message boundaries are preserved, and so on. The constant SOCK_STREAM specifies a socket with reliable byte-stream semantics, whereas SOCK_DGRAM specifies a best-effort datagram socket.

The third parameter specifies the particular *end-to-end protocol* to be used. For the PF_INET protocol family, we want TCP (identified by the constant IPPROTO_TCP) for a stream socket and UDP (identified by IPPROTO_UDP) for a datagram socket. Supplying the constant 0 as the third parameter requests the *default* end-to-end protocol for the specified protocol

9

family and type. Because there is currently only one choice for stream and datagram sockets in the TCP/IP protocol family, we could specify 0 instead of giving the protocol number explicitly. Someday, however, there might be other end-to-end protocols in the Internet protocol family that implement the same semantics. In that case, specifying 0 might result in the use of a different protocol, which might or might not be desirable. The main thing is to ensure that the communicating programs are using the same end-to-end protocol.

The return value of socket() is actually an integer: a nonnegative value for success and −1 for failure. A nonfailure value should be treated as an opaque handle, like a file descriptor. (In reality, it *is* a file descriptor, taken from the same space as the numbers returned by open().) This handle, which we call a *socket descriptor,* is passed to other API functions to identify the socket abstraction on which the operation is to be carried out.

When an application is finished with a socket, it calls close(), giving the descriptor for the socket that is no longer needed.

---

int close(**int** *socket*)

---

close() tells the underlying protocol stack to initiate any actions required to shut down communications and deallocate any resources associated with the socket. close() returns 0 on success or −1 on failure. Once close() has been called, it is not possible to send or receive data through the socket.

2.2 Specifying Addresses

Applications using sockets need to be able to specify Internet addresses and ports to the kernel. For example, a client must specify the address of the server application with which it needs to communicate. In addition, the sockets layer sometimes needs to pass addresses to the application. For example, a feature analogous to "Caller ID" in the telephone network enables a server to learn the address of each client that communicates with it.

The sockets API defines a generic data type—the **sockaddr** structure—for specifying addresses associated with sockets:

```
struct sockaddr
{
    unsigned short sa_family;  /* Address family (e.g. AF_INET) */
    char sa_data[14];          /* Family-specific address information */
};
```

The first part of this address structure defines the address family—the space to which the address belongs. For our purposes, we will always use the constant AF_INET, which specifies the Internet address family. The second part is a blob of bits whose exact form depends on the address family. This is a typical way of dealing with heterogeneity in operating systems and

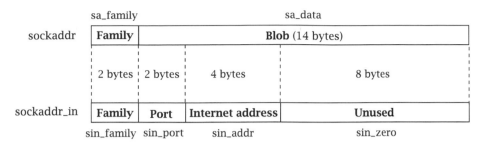

Figure 2.1: Address structures.

networking. As we discussed in Section 1.2, socket addresses have two parts: a 32-bit Internet address and a 16-bit port number.

Recall that when specifying the protocol family to socket(), we use PF_INET for the Internet protocol family. The designers of the sockets API wanted to provide maximum flexibility; they envisioned the possibility that one protocol family might have many different addressing schemes. Therefore, they allowed for protocol families and address families to be independent of each other. In practice, there is only one address family per protocol family. In fact, the AF_*xxx* and PF_*xxx* constants have historically been interchangeable (e.g., AF_INET has the same value as PF_INET). When talking about protocol and address families, we always use PF_INET and AF_INET, respectively.

The particular form of the **sockaddr** structure that is used for TCP/IP socket addresses is the **sockaddr_in** structure.

```
struct in_addr
{
    unsigned long s_addr;        /* Internet address (32 bits) */
};

struct sockaddr_in
{
    unsigned short sin_family; /* Internet protocol (AF_INET) */
    unsigned short sin_port;   /* Address port (16 bits) */
    struct in_addr sin_addr;   /* Internet address (32 bits) */
    char sin_zero[8];          /* Not used */
};
```

As you can see, the **sockaddr_in** structure has fields for the port number and Internet address in addition to the address family. It is important to understand that **sockaddr_in** is just another view of the data in a **sockaddr** structure, tailored to sockets using the Internet protocols, as shown in Figure 2.1. Thus, we can fill in the fields of a **sockaddr_in** and then cast it to a **sockaddr** to pass it to the socket functions, which look at the sa_family field to learn how the rest of the address is structured.

2.3 TCP Client

The distinction between client and server is important because each uses the sockets interface differently at certain steps in the communication. We first focus on the client. Its job is to initiate communication with a server that is passively waiting to be contacted. The setup for a TCP and UDP client is very similar; however, there are differences in the semantics of sending and receiving, which we address in Chapter 4. For now, we focus on TCP because sending and receiving over a TCP socket is most similar to file I/O.

The typical TCP client goes through four basic steps:

1. Create a TCP socket using socket().

2. Establish a connection to the server using connect().

3. Communicate using send() and recv().

4. Close the connection with close().

We have already described the process of socket creation and closing. To get a TCP socket, we supply PF_INET, SOCK_STREAM, and IPPROTO_TCP as the parameters to socket().

A TCP socket must be connected to another socket before any data can be sent through it. In this sense using TCP sockets is something like using the telephone network. Before you can talk, you have to specify the number you want, and a connection must be established; if the connection cannot be established, you have to try again later. The connection establishment process is the biggest difference between clients and servers: The client initiates the connection while the server waits passively for clients to connect to it. (For additional details about the connection process and how it relates to the API functions, see Section 6.4.) To establish a connection with the server, we call connect() on the socket.

---

int connect(**int** *socket*, **struct sockaddr** **foreignAddress*, **unsigned int** *addressLength*)

---

socket is the descriptor created by socket(). *foreignAddress* is declared to be a pointer to a **sockaddr** because the sockets API is generic; for our purposes, it will always be a pointer to a **sockaddr_in** containing the Internet address and port of the server. *addressLength* specifies the length of the address structure and is invariably given as sizeof(struct sockaddr_in). When connect() returns, the socket is connected and communication can proceed with calls to send() and recv().

---

int send(**int** *socket*, **const void** **msg*, **unsigned int** *msgLength*, **int** *flags*)
int recv(**int** *socket*, **void** **rcvBuffer*, **unsigned int** *bufferLength*, **int** *flags*)

---

send() and recv() have very similar arguments. *socket* is the descriptor for the connected socket through which data is to be sent or received. For send(), *msg* points to the message to send, and *msgLength* is the length (bytes) of the message. The default behavior for send() is to block until all of the data is sent (we describe this process more precisely in Chapter 6). For recv(), *rcvBuffer* points to the buffer—that is, an area in memory such as a character array—where received data will be placed, and *bufferLength* gives the length of the buffer, which is the maximum number of bytes that can be received at once. The default behavior for recv() is to block until at least some bytes can be transferred.

The *flags* parameter in both send() and recv() provides a way to change the default behavior of the socket call. Setting *flags* to 0 specifies the default behavior. send() and recv() return the number of bytes sent or received or −1 for failure. Finally, to terminate the connection, the client calls close().

Our first example application, called TCPEchoClient.c, is a client that communicates with an "echo" server using TCP. Many systems include such a server for debugging and testing purposes; the server simply echoes whatever it receives back to the client. The string to be echoed is provided as a command-line argument to our client.

TCPEchoClient.c

```
0   #include <stdio.h>        /* for printf() and fprintf() */
1   #include <sys/socket.h>   /* for socket(), connect(), send(), and recv() */
2   #include <arpa/inet.h>    /* for sockaddr_in and inet_addr() */
3   #include <stdlib.h>       /* for atoi() */
4   #include <string.h>       /* for memset() */
5   #include <unistd.h>       /* for close() */
6
7   #define RCVBUFSIZE 32     /* Size of receive buffer */
8
9   void DieWithError(char *errorMessage);  /* Error handling function */
10
11  int main(int argc, char *argv[])
12  {
13      int sock;                       /* Socket descriptor */
14      struct sockaddr_in echoServAddr; /* Echo server address */
15      unsigned short echoServPort;     /* Echo server port */
16      char *servIP;                    /* Server IP address (dotted quad) */
17      char *echoString;                /* String to send to echo server */
18      char echoBuffer[RCVBUFSIZE];     /* Buffer for echo string */
19      unsigned int echoStringLen;      /* Length of string to echo */
20      int bytesRcvd, totalBytesRcvd;   /* Bytes read in single recv()
21                                          and total bytes read */
22
23      if ((argc < 3) || (argc > 4))    /* Test for correct number of arguments */
24      {
25          fprintf(stderr, "Usage: %s <Server IP> <Echo Word> [<Echo Port>]\n",
26                  argv[0]);
27          exit(1);
28      }
```

```
29
30       servIP = argv[1];              /* First arg: server IP address (dotted quad) */
31       echoString = argv[2];          /* Second arg: string to echo */
32
33       if (argc == 4)
34           echoServPort = atoi(argv[3]); /* Use given port, if any */
35       else
36           echoServPort = 7;   /* 7 is the well-known port for the echo service */
37
38       /* Create a reliable, stream socket using TCP */
39       if ((sock = socket(PF_INET, SOCK_STREAM, IPPROTO_TCP)) < 0)
40           DieWithError("socket() failed");
41
42       /* Construct the server address structure */
43       memset(&echoServAddr, 0, sizeof(echoServAddr));    /* Zero out structure */
44       echoServAddr.sin_family      = AF_INET;              /* Internet address family */
45       echoServAddr.sin_addr.s_addr = inet_addr(servIP);   /* Server IP address */
46       echoServAddr.sin_port        = htons(echoServPort); /* Server port */
47
48       /* Establish the connection to the echo server */
49       if (connect(sock, (struct sockaddr *) &echoServAddr, sizeof(echoServAddr)) < 0)
50           DieWithError("connect() failed");
51
52       echoStringLen = strlen(echoString);          /* Determine input length */
53
54       /* Send the string to the server */
55       if (send(sock, echoString, echoStringLen, 0) != echoStringLen)
56           DieWithError("send() sent a different number of bytes than expected");
57
58       /* receive the same string back from the server */
59       totalBytesRcvd = 0;
60       printf("Received: ");                    /* Setup to print the echoed string */
61       while (totalBytesRcvd < echoStringLen)
62       {
63           /* Receive up to the buffer size (minus 1 to leave space for
64              a null terminator) bytes from the sender */
65           if ((bytesRcvd = recv(sock, echoBuffer, RCVBUFSIZE - 1, 0)) <= 0)
66               DieWithError("recv() failed or connection closed prematurely");
67           totalBytesRcvd += bytesRcvd;   /* Keep tally of total bytes */
68           echoBuffer[bytesRcvd] = '\0';  /* Terminate the string! */
69           printf(echoBuffer);            /* Print the echo buffer */
70       }
71
72       printf("\n");    /* Print a final linefeed */
73
```

```
74      close(sock);
75      exit(0);
76  }
```

`TCPEchoClient.c` goes through six steps:

1. **Application setup and parameter parsing:** lines 0–36

   - **Include files:** lines 0–5
   These header files declare the standard functions and constants of the API. Consult your documentation (e.g., man pages) for the appropriate include files for socket functions and data structures on your system.
   - **Declaration of application-specific variables and constants:** lines 7, 13–20
   - **Typical parameter parsing and sanity checking:** lines 23–36

2. **TCP socket creation:** lines 39–40

3. **Echo server address specification and connection establishment:** lines 43–50

   - `memset()`: line 43
   The echo server's Internet address and port are passed to `connect()` in a **sockaddr_in** structure. The call to `memset()` ensures that, after the **sockaddr_in** structure is filled in with the desired values, the extra bytes in the structure contain zero. (This step is needed on some systems, but not all.)
   - **Filling in the sockaddr_in:** lines 44–46
   We must set the address family (AF_INET), Internet address, and port number. The function `inet_addr()` converts the string representation of the server's Internet address (expected in dotted-quad format) into a 32-bit binary representation. Note that we assign the return value to the only member of the **struct in_addr** address field. Finally, the server's port number is an optional command-line argument; if it is not specified by the user, the well-known port number for the echo service (7) is used as the default. In any case, the port number was converted to the appropriate type earlier; the call to `htons()` is required because of byte-ordering issues (of which we postpone discussion until Chapter 3).
   - **Connecting:** lines 49–50
   `connect()` establishes the connection between this socket and the socket specified by the address and port in the **sockaddr_in** structure. Because the sockets API is generic, the pointer to the **sockaddr_in** address structure needs to be cast to the generic type (**sockaddr**), and the actual size of the address data structure must be supplied.

4. **Send echo string to server:** lines 52–56

We pass a pointer to the echo string parameter in the send() call; it was stored somewhere (like all command-line arguments) when the application was started. We do not really care where it is, we just need to know the address of the first byte to send and how many bytes the string contains. Note that we do not send the termination character ('\0').

5. **Receive echo server reply:** lines 59–72

TCP is a byte-stream protocol. One implication of this type of protocol is that send() boundaries are not preserved. The bytes sent by a call to send() on one end of a connection may not all be returned by a single call to recv() on the other end. (We discuss this issue in more detail in Chapters 3 and 6.) Therefore, we repeatedly receive bytes until we have received as many as we sent. In all likelihood, this loop will only be executed once because the data from the server will be returned all at once; however, that is not *guaranteed* to happen, and so we have to allow for the possibility that multiple reads are required.

■ **Receive a block of bytes:** lines 65–67

recv() blocks until data is available, returning the number of bytes copied into the buffer or −1 in case of failure. A return value of zero indicates that the application at the other end closed the TCP connection. Note that the size parameter passed to recv() reserves space for a terminating null character, so printf() can find the end of the string.

■ **Print buffer:** lines 68–69

We print the data sent by the server as it is received. We add the terminating null character (\0) at the end of each chunk of received data so that it can be treated as a string by printf(). We do not check whether the bytes received are the same as the bytes sent. The server may send something completely different (up to the length of the string we sent), and it will be written to the standard output.

■ **Print newline:** line 72

When we have received as many bytes as we sent, we exit the loop and print a newline.

6. **Terminate connection and exit:** lines 74–75

Our applications use a standard error function, DieWithError(**char** *errorMessage*). DieWithError() outputs a caller-specified error string, followed by an error description string from the system based on the value of the special variable *errno* (which describes the reason for the most recent failure, if any, of a system call), and exits the application with a nonzero return code. DieWithError.c should be compiled and linked with *all* other example applications in this text.

DieWithError.c

```
0  #include <stdio.h>  /* for perror() */
1  #include <stdlib.h> /* for exit() */
```

```
2
3  void DieWithError(char *errorMessage)
4  {
5      perror(errorMessage);
6      exit(1);
7  }
```

DieWithError.c

If we compile this application as TCPEchoClient, we can communicate with an echo server with Internet address 169.1.1.1 as follows:

```
% TCPEchoClient 169.1.1.1 "Echo this!"
Received: Echo this!
```

2.4 TCP Server

We now turn our focus to constructing a server. The server's job is to set up a communication endpoint and passively wait for a connection from the client. As with clients, the setup for a TCP and UDP server is similar. For now we focus on a TCP server and discuss the differences of a UDP server in Chapter 4. There are four steps for TCP server communication:

1. Create a TCP socket using socket().
2. Assign a port number to the socket with bind().
3. Tell the system to allow connections to be made to that port, using listen().
4. Repeatedly do the following:
   - Call accept() to get a new socket for each client connection.
   - Communicate with the client via that new socket using send() and recv().
   - Close the client connection using close().

Creating the socket, sending, receiving, and closing are the same as in the client. The differences in the server have to do with binding an address to the socket and then using the socket as a channel to "receive" other sockets that are connected to clients.

For the client to contact the server, the server's socket must have an assigned local address and port; the function that accomplishes this is bind(). Notice that while the client has to supply the server's address to connect(), the server has to specify its own address to bind(). It is this piece of information (i.e., the server's address and port) that they have to agree on to communicate; neither one really needs to know the client's address.

int bind(**int** *socket*, **struct sockaddr** **localAddress*, **unsigned int** *addressLength*)

The first parameter is the descriptor returned by an earlier call to socket(). As with connect(), the address parameter is declared as a pointer to a **sockaddr**, but for TCP/IP applications, it will actually point to a **sockaddr_in** containing the Internet address of the local interface and the port to listen on. *addressLength* is the length of the address structure, invariably passed as sizeof(struct sockaddr_in). bind() returns 0 on success and −1 on failure. If successful, the socket identified by the given descriptor (and no other) is associated with the given Internet address and port. The Internet address can be set to the special wildcard value INADDR_ANY, which means that connections to the specified port will be directed to this socket, regardless of which Internet address they are sent to; this practice can be useful if the host happens to have multiple Internet addresses.

Now that the socket has an address (or at least a port), we need to instruct the underlying TCP protocol implementation to listen for connections from clients by calling listen() on the socket.

---

int listen(**int** *socket*, **int** *queueLimit*)

---

listen() causes internal state changes to the given socket, so that incoming TCP connection requests will be handled and then queued for acceptance by the program. The *queueLimit* parameter specifies an upper bound on the number of incoming connections that can be waiting at any time. (Actually, the precise effect of *queueLimit* is very system dependent, so consult your system's technical specifications.) listen() returns 0 on success and −1 on failure.

At first it might seem that a server should now wait for a connection on the socket that it has set up, send and receive through that socket, close it, and then repeat the process. However, that is not the way it works. The socket that has been bound to a port and marked "listening" is never actually used for sending and receiving. Instead, it is used as a way of getting *new* sockets, one for each client connection; the server then sends and receives on the *new* sockets. The server gets a socket for an incoming client connection by calling accept().

---

int accept(**int** *socket*, **struct sockaddr** **clientAddress*, **unsigned int** **addressLength*)

---

accept() dequeues the next connection on the queue for *socket*. If the queue is empty, accept() blocks until a connection request arrives. When successful, accept() fills in the **sockaddr** structure, pointed to by *clientAddress*, with the address of the client at the other end of the connection. *addressLength* specifies the maximum size of the *clientAddress* address structure and contains the number of bytes actually used for the address upon return.

If successful, accept() returns a descriptor for a *new* socket that is connected to the client. The socket sent as the first parameter to accept() is unchanged (not connected to the client) and continues to listen for new connection requests. On failure, accept() returns −1. The server communicates with the client using send() and recv(); when communication is complete, the connection is terminated with a call to close().

Our next example program, TCPEchoServer.c, implements the echo service used by our client program. The server is simple. Like most servers, it runs forever, doing the following: (1) it sets up a listening socket and waits for an incoming connection from a client; (2) when one arrives, it repeatedly receives bytes and sends them again until the client terminates the connection, and (3) it closes the client connection.

TCPEchoServer.c

```
0   #include <stdio.h>       /* for printf() and fprintf() */
1   #include <sys/socket.h>  /* for socket(), bind(), and connect() */
2   #include <arpa/inet.h>   /* for sockaddr_in and inet_ntoa() */
3   #include <stdlib.h>      /* for atoi() */
4   #include <string.h>      /* for memset() */
5   #include <unistd.h>      /* for close() */
6
7   #define MAXPENDING 5     /* Maximum outstanding connection requests */
8
9   void DieWithError(char *errorMessage);  /* Error handling function */
10  void HandleTCPClient(int clntSocket);   /* TCP client handling function */
11
12  int main(int argc, char *argv[])
13  {
14      int servSock;                    /* Socket descriptor for server */
15      int clntSock;                    /* Socket descriptor for client */
16      struct sockaddr_in echoServAddr; /* Local address */
17      struct sockaddr_in echoClntAddr; /* Client address */
18      unsigned short echoServPort;     /* Server port */
19      unsigned int clntLen;            /* Length of client address data structure */
20
21      if (argc != 2)     /* Test for correct number of arguments */
22      {
23          fprintf(stderr, "Usage:  %s <Server Port>\n", argv[0]);
24          exit(1);
25      }
26
27      echoServPort = atoi(argv[1]);  /* First arg:  local port */
28
29      /* Create socket for incoming connections */
30      if ((servSock = socket(PF_INET, SOCK_STREAM, IPPROTO_TCP)) < 0)
31          DieWithError("socket() failed");
32
33      /* Construct local address structure */
34      memset(&echoServAddr, 0, sizeof(echoServAddr));   /* Zero out structure */
35      echoServAddr.sin_family = AF_INET;                /* Internet address family */
36      echoServAddr.sin_addr.s_addr = htonl(INADDR_ANY); /* Any incoming interface */
37      echoServAddr.sin_port = htons(echoServPort);      /* Local port */
```

```
38
39          /* Bind to the local address */
40          if (bind(servSock, (struct sockaddr *) &echoServAddr, sizeof(echoServAddr)) < 0)
41              DieWithError("bind() failed");
42
43          /* Mark the socket so it will listen for incoming connections */
44          if (listen(servSock, MAXPENDING) < 0)
45              DieWithError("listen() failed");
46
47          for (;;) /* Run forever */
48          {
49              /* Set the size of the in-out parameter */
50              clntLen = sizeof(echoClntAddr);
51
52              /* Wait for a client to connect */
53              if ((clntSock = accept(servSock, (struct sockaddr *) &echoClntAddr,
54                                  &clntLen)) < 0)
55                  DieWithError("accept() failed");
56
57              /* clntSock is connected to a client! */
58
59              printf("Handling client %s\n", inet_ntoa(echoClntAddr.sin_addr));
60
61              HandleTCPClient(clntSock);
62          }
63          /* NOT REACHED */
64  }
```

TCPEchoServer.c

1. **Program setup and parameter parsing:** lines 0–27

2. **Socket creation and setup:** lines 30–41

   - **Create a TCP socket:** lines 30–31
     Again we create a stream socket and specify TCP as the protocol.

   - **Fill in local address:** lines 34–37
     We use a **sockaddr_in** structure to specify the local Internet address and port number for this server. We specify the wildcard INADDR_ANY as the Internet address. This is usually the right thing to do for servers, and it saves us from having to find out the host's actual Internet address. The port number to use is specified on the command line. We convert both the address and port to network byte order using htonl() and htons() (see Section 3.2).

   - **Bind socket to specified address and port number:** lines 40–41
     bind() fills in the local address and port number associated with the specified socket.

bind() may fail for various reasons; one of the most important is that some other socket is already bound to the specified port (see Section 6.5). Also, on some systems special privileges are required to bind to port numbers less than 1024 because they are the well-known ports.

■ **Set the socket to listen:** lines 44-45
listen() informs the TCP implementation to allow incoming connections from clients. Before the call to listen(), any incoming connection requests to the socket's address would be rejected—the client's connect() would fail.

3. **Iteratively handle incoming connections:** lines 47-62

■ **Accept an incoming connection:** lines 50-55
As discussed above, a TCP socket on which listen() has been called is used differently than the one we saw in the client application. Instead of sending and receiving on the socket, the server application calls accept(), which blocks until an incoming connection is made to the listening socket's port number. accept() then returns a descriptor for a new socket, which is already connected to the initiating remote socket. The second argument points to a **sockaddr_in** structure, and the third argument is a pointer to the length of that structure. Upon success, the **sockaddr_in** contains the Internet address and port of the client to which the returned socket is connected; the address's length has been written into the integer pointed to by the third argument. Note that the socket referenced by the returned descriptor is already *connected*; among other things this means it is ready for reading and writing.

■ **Report connected client:** line 59
echoClntAddr contains the address of the connecting client; we provide a "Caller ID" function and print out the client's information. inet_ntoa() is the inverse of inet_addr(), which we used in the client. It takes the 32-bit binary representation of the client's address and converts it to a dotted-quad string.

■ **Handle echo client:** line 61
HandleTCPClient() receives the echo message and echoes it back to the client.

HandleTCPClient() receives data on the given socket and sends it back on the same socket, iterating as long as recv() returns a positive value (indicating that something was received). recv() blocks until something is received or the client closes the connection. When the client closes the connection normally, recv() returns 0.

HandleTCPClient.c

```
0  #include <stdio.h>       /* for printf() and fprintf() */
1  #include <sys/socket.h> /* for recv() and send() */
2  #include <unistd.h>      /* for close() */
3
4  #define RCVBUFSIZE 32    /* Size of receive buffer */
5
```

```
 6  void DieWithError(char *errorMessage);   /* Error handling function */
 7
 8  void HandleTCPClient(int clntSocket)
 9  {
10      char echoBuffer[RCVBUFSIZE];         /* Buffer for echo string */
11      int recvMsgSize;                     /* Size of received message */
12
13      /* Receive message from client */
14      if ((recvMsgSize = recv(clntSocket, echoBuffer, RCVBUFSIZE, 0)) < 0)
15          DieWithError("recv() failed");
16
17      /* Send received string and receive again until end of transmission */
18      while (recvMsgSize > 0)      /* zero indicates end of transmission */
19      {
20          /* Echo message back to client */
21          if (send(clntSocket, echoBuffer, recvMsgSize, 0) != recvMsgSize)
22              DieWithError("send() failed");
23
24          /* See if there is more data to receive */
25          if ((recvMsgSize = recv(clntSocket, echoBuffer, RCVBUFSIZE, 0)) < 0)
26              DieWithError("recv() failed");
27      }
28
29      close(clntSocket);    /* Close client socket */
30  }
```

_____

HandleTCPClient.c

If we compile the server as TCPEchoServer and use our client to connect to it, their outputs will be as follows:

TCP Echo Server on a host with Internet address 169.1.1.1 and port 5000

```
% TCPEchoServer 5000
Handling client 169.1.1.2
```

TCP Echo Client on a host with Internet address 169.1.1.2

```
% TCPEchoClient 169.1.1.1 "Echo this!" 5000
Received: Echo this!
```

The server binds its socket to port 5000 and waits for a connection request from the client. The client connects, sends the message "Echo this!" to the server, and receives the echoed response. In this execution, we have to supply TCPEchoClient with the port number on the command line because it is talking to our echo server, which is on port 5000 rather than the well-known port 7.

Thought Questions

1. For TCPEchoServer.c we explicitly provide an address to the socket using bind(). We said that a socket must have an address for communication, yet we do not perform a bind() in TCPEchoClient.c. How is the echo client's socket given a local address?

2. (Suggested by Ted Herman) When you make a phone call, it's usually the callee that answers with "Hello." What changes to our example client and server would be needed to implement this?

3. Servers are supposed to run for a long time without stopping. Therefore, they have to be designed to provide good service no matter what their clients do. Examine the example TCPEchoServer.c and list anything you can think of that a client might do to cause the server to give poor service to other clients. Suggest improvements to fix the problems you find.

chapter 3

Constructing Messages

When writing programs to use the sockets interface, you will often be implementing an *application protocol* of some sort. Typically, you use a socket because your program needs to provide information to, or use information provided by, another program. There is no magic: Sender and receiver must agree on how this information will be encoded, who sends what information when, and how the communication will be terminated. In the examples we have seen so far, the application protocol is rather trivial because the echo clients and servers pay no attention to the data itself but simply count bytes to determine what to do next. Most applications that use sockets are more complicated. This chapter discusses some basics of data encoding; it is intended to help you avoid some of the common pitfalls of formatting and parsing messages.

The TCP/IP protocols transport bytes of user data without examining or modifying them. This service allows applications great flexibility in how they encode their information for transmission. For various reasons, most application protocols are defined in terms of discrete *messages* made up of *fields*; each field contains a specific piece of information. The application protocol needs to specify how the data will be formatted by the sender so that the receiver can parse it into its components and extract the meaning of those components.

For example, consider a program that needs to send two numbers to another program. Suppose the first number represents the total amount of money deposited into a bank on a particular day, and the second number represents the total amount withdrawn on that same day. To keep things simple, let's assume that the unit of money is the penny and that the numbers are integers. The sending and receiving programs need to agree on how these two numbers (among other things) will be represented—otherwise the bank will have problems!

We will be dealing with the bank example in the rest of this chapter, and the following assumptions will apply:

- The two amounts in question are stored in the sending program in program variables (of type **int**) called *deposits* and *withdrawals*.

- The **int** *s* contains the descriptor for the (TCP) socket to be used for the communication.

■ For the machine and compiler in use, sizeof(**int**) is 4, and sizeof(**short**) is 2.

Although the examples in this chapter use TCP (send() and recv()), most of this chapter applies equally well to UDP; exceptions are noted as such.

3.1 Encoding Data

One way to represent the withdrawal and deposit information is to encode the numbers as strings of printable decimal digits, that is, sequences of bytes whose values are determined according to a *character encoding* such as ASCII. This method has the advantage that it is the same representation you would use if you were printing the numbers or displaying them in a window on the screen. Also, representing numbers as strings of digits allows you to send arbitrarily large numbers, at least in principle.

Using this kind of encoding, the message would contain two fields; each field would consist of a string of ASCII digits (i.e., bytes containing values in the range 48, which represents '0', through 57, which represents '9') followed by a *delimiter*. The delimiter of each field could in principle be any value not in the range '0'–'9' but in practice would probably be either a null byte (for consistency with C's string representation method) or a byte of *white space*, that is, a character like space or tab (for readability by humans). The first field is designated as the value of *deposits* and the second as the value of *withdrawals*.

If the two amounts are 17,998,720 and 47,034,615, respectively, and the ASCII space character (decimal byte value 32) is used as the delimiter, the two numbers would be encoded as the following sequence of (decimal) byte values (each byte contains a number from 0 to 255, the largest binary value representable in 8 bits):

49	55	57	57	56	55	50	48	32	52	55	48	51	52	54	49	53	32
'1'	'7'	'9'	'9'	'8'	'7'	'2'	'0'	' '	'4'	'7'	'0'	'3'	'4'	'6'	'1'	'5'	' '

Thus, if the message contained nothing else besides these two fields, it would be exactly 18 bytes long. The sending program can construct and send such a message as follows:

```
sprintf(msgBuffer, "%d %d ", deposits, withdrawals);
send(s, msgBuffer, strlen(msgBuffer), 0);
```

There are several potential pitfalls to be aware of here. First, note the space character at the end of the format string passed to sprintf(); it is required by the protocol because, without it, the withdrawal number will not be delimited, and the receiving program may not be able to separate it from whatever follows it. (Receiver parsing is discussed further in Section 3.4.)

Second, *msgBuffer* needs to be big enough to hold the biggest possible result (all digits in the two numbers, plus the sign characters (in case the numbers are negative), plus the two spaces, plus the terminating null character. If the numbers are nine digits each, the buffer needs to have at least 23 bytes. If it is not big enough, the program may crash, or, even worse, it may silently overwrite some other data in the program. The moral here is that *the use of* sprintf() *requires careful planning!*

Third, notice that the third argument to send() counts *only* the bytes that make up the two fields of the message. In particular, it does not send the null at the end of the string nor any of the bytes in *msgBuf* that may be beyond the end of the message. A common mistake among novices is to send the entire array, independent of the formatted length of the message fields, like this:

```
#define BUFSIZE 132
    .
    .
    .
char msgBuf[BUFSIZE];
    .
    .
    .
sprintf(msgBuffer, "%d %d ", deposits, withdrawals);
send(s, msgBuffer, BUFSIZE, 0);
```

This method is wrong,[1] because the receiving program will receive the extra bytes beyond the second space—and depending on how *msgBuf* is declared (global or local to some function), and how it has been used earlier in the program, those bytes may contain garbage.

One disadvantage of encoding numbers as text strings is that it is not very efficient: Each byte in the digit string will contain one of 10 values, but choosing among 10 values can be done using four bits or less. Moreover, it is inconvenient to *manipulate* numbers encoded in this way inside the program. For example, if the receiving program needed to find out how much the net deposits of the bank increased or decreased on this day, it would need to convert both amounts to native integer representation (for whatever machine it was running on), so that it could subtract the number representing withdrawals from the number representing deposits, using the integer subtraction operator. (C has no "subtraction" operator for text strings.)

It is an unfortunate fact of life that native (say, 32-bit or 64-bit) binary representations of integers impose fixed limits on the size of numbers that can be represented. For example, on a 32-bit two's-complement machine the largest positive integer that can be represented natively is 2,147,483,647. So the advantage of being able to represent arbitrarily large numbers as text strings is moot if you ultimately need to be able to convert them to/from a native representation. Nevertheless, if we can guarantee that the numbers we want to send will not exceed some value, we can eliminate the conversion on each end by sending the values of *deposits* and *withdrawals* as binary numbers. This encoding is usually more efficient in terms of the number of bytes used to represent a number but has its own pitfalls arising from the possibility that the sender and receiver may have different native integer formats. Therefore, the protocol must say specifically how many bits (or bytes) are used for each integer and what kind of encoding is used (e.g., two's complement, sign/magnitude, or unsigned).

---

[1] Unless the numbers both happen to be 65 digits long, and even then it would not be correct, just lucky.

Returning to our example, if we knew somehow that a single day's withdrawals or deposits would not exceed $21,474,836.47, then we could design the protocol so that the message containing deposits and withdrawals would consist of two fields of 32 bits (4 bytes) each.

Now a typical way for the sender to construct the message would use a structure; the code would look something like this:

```
struct {
    int dep;
    int wd;
} msgStruct;
    .
    .
    msgStruct.dep = deposits;
    msgStruct.wd = withdrawals;
    send(s, &msgStruct, sizeof(msgStruct), 0);
```

Of course, because we are using TCP, we can simply send the values of *deposits* and *withdrawals* without first copying them into a structure:

```
send(s, &deposits, sizeof(deposits), 0);
send(s, &withdrawals, sizeof(withdrawals), 0);
```

With UDP this does not work because it results in two separate datagrams.

In each case, the sequence of bytes sent is the same: the four bytes that make up the integer *deposits*, followed by the four bytes that make up *withdrawals*. There is, however, a potential problem with the above code, which again arises from the differences between different machines' representation of integers. The next section deals with this problem.

3.2 Byte Ordering

Suppose that the value of the **int** *deposits* is 17,998,720 and *withdrawals* is 47,034,615. The problem of byte ordering is illustrated by the msgStruct code above. The sequence of bytes sent as a result of that code depends upon the architecture of the machine on which the code is executed. On a so-called Big-Endian machine, the sequence will be

1	18	163	128	2	205	176	247

(where again the contents of each byte are represented as a decimal number). On such machines the *most-significant byte* of a word (of any size) has the lowest address, that is, the same address as the word itself. On a so-called Little-Endian machine, the bytes sent would be

128	163	18	1	247	176	205	2

That is, the bytes within the two integers occur in opposite order from that on the Big-Endian machine, because the *least-significant byte* has the same address as the word on such machines. Examples of Big-Endian architectures include the Motorola 68000 family and Sparc; among the Little-Endians are the Intel x86 and DEC Alpha architectures.[2] The point is that when you transfer a multibyte structure—a native integer or anything more complex—using the sockets interface, the bytes within the structure are sent in order of ascending byte address. Similarly, on the receiving machine, the bytes will be placed into memory in ascending-address order as they are received.

Now consider what happens when the sending program has the opposite byte ordering from the receiving program, which receives the data into a buffer like

```
struct {
  int deposits;
  int withdrawals;
} rcvBuf;
    .
    .
    .
/* receive 2*sizeof(int) bytes into rcvBuf... */
```

For the values given above, the receiver would interpret the deposits number as −2,136,796,671 and the withdrawals number as −139,408,126, which should give you an idea of why this problem is an important one.

Fortunately, there is a simple solution that works in almost all cases. By convention, the standard "network byte order" is Big-Endian, and standard routines are provided to convert two- and four-byte integers from native to network byte order. The function htonl(x) ("host to network long") returns the result of converting the given four-byte value from native byte order to network byte order. (If the native byte order is the same as network byte order, the conversion function is a no-op. These functions may be defined as macros.) Similarly, htons() converts a two-byte (short) value to network order and returns the result, and ntohl() and ntohs() convert values from network to host (native) byte order.

---

long int htonl(**long int** *hostLong*)
short int htons(**short int** *hostShort*)
long int ntohl(**long int** *netLong*)
short int ntohs(**short int** *netShort*)

Whenever you send a *multibyte, binary* value from one machine to another, you need to use the hton*() routines. In addition, any time you pass externally significant values (i.e., Internet addresses and ports) to an API function in a **sockaddr** structure, *the implementation*

---

[2] Though there once were other possibilities besides Big- and Little-Endian, today virtually all machines are one or the other, and some, like the PowerPC, are configurable to operate in either mode.

expects those values to be in network byte order. In general, you should apply these conversions as the last operation before sending the data and as the first operation after receiving it.

The correct code for the sender (assuming four-byte integers) is

```
msgStruct.dep = htonl(deposits);
msgStruct.wd = htonl(withdrawals);
send(s, &msgStruct, sizeof(msgStruct), 0);
```

Similarly, the receiver needs to convert the values before using them, that is, to call `ntohl()` on each integer value before using it.

3.3   Alignment and Padding

When messages contain multiple binary-encoded fields of different sizes, we must take account of *alignment* considerations in defining the protocol. Continuing with our bank example, suppose that in addition to the number of pennies deposited and withdrawn, we want the message to contain the number of deposit and withdrawal transactions. Let's assume further that we know that there will never be more than 65,535 transactions of either type in a single day. This means that we can represent the transaction counts as two-byte, unsigned integers (i.e., **unsigned short**s) in the message.

We want the message to consist of the four-byte deposits amount in network byte order, followed by the two-byte number of deposits in network byte order, followed by the four-byte withdrawals amount, followed by the two-byte number of withdrawals:

cents deposited	# of deposits	cents withdrawn	# of withdrawals
4 bytes	2 bytes	4 bytes	2 bytes

Thus, we want the total size of the message to be 12 (= 4 + 2 + 4 + 2) bytes. Now suppose we construct and send the message using a structure, like this:

```
struct {
  int centsDeposited;
  unsigned short numDeps;
  int centsWithdrawn;
  unsigned short numWds;
} msgBuf;
 :
 :   /* assign values to fields -- convert byte order! */
send(s, &msgBuf, sizeof(msgBuf), 0);
```

Unfortunately, on some machines this code will not produce a 12-byte message but rather a 14-byte message, which contains two extra *padding* bytes between numDeps and centsWithdrawn. The reason for this addition is that the compiler aligns the fields of structures to certain word boundaries based on their type. The main things you need to remember to understand alignment are the following:

- Data structures are maximally aligned, that is, their addresses will be divisible by the size of the largest native integer.

- Other multibyte fields are aligned to their size, that is, a four-byte integer's address will be divisible by four, and a two-byte integer's address will be divisible by two.

Thus, the address of the variable *msgBuf* will be divisible by four, as will the address of the field centsWithdrawn. Because the next available byte after the numDeps field is aligned on a two-byte but not a four-byte boundary, the compiler adds two padding bytes so that centsWithdrawn is aligned on a four-byte boundary.

centsDeposited	numDeps	[pad]	centsWithdrawn	NumWds
4 bytes	2 bytes	2 bytes	4 bytes	2 bytes

The way to get around the addition of padding is to define the protocol message so that all fields are aligned properly. This can be done either by (1) including the padding in the message definition explicitly or (2) rearranging the fields so they are aligned. For our example we choose (2) and define the message as

centsDeposited	centsWithdrawn	numDeps	numWds
4 bytes	4 bytes	2 bytes	2 bytes

and declare the structure as

```
struct MsgBuf {
  int centsDeposited;
  int centsWithdrawn;
  unsigned short numDeps;
  unsigned short numWds;
} msgBuf;
```

Now we have sizeof(*msgBuf*)=12, as desired.

3.4 Framing and Parsing

Application protocols typically deal with discrete messages, which are viewed as collections of fields. *Framing* is the problem of formatting the information so that the receiver can parse messages (i.e., locate the beginning and end of the message and the boundaries between fields within the message). Whether information is encoded as human-readable text or machine-manipulable binary words, the application protocol must enable the receiver of a message to determine that it has received all of a transmitted message.

If the fields in a message have fixed sizes and the size of the message is known in advance, the receiver can simply receive the expected number of bytes into a buffer. For the example message above that had four fields (deposits, withdrawals, and the number of each type of transaction), the receiving program can declare a variable of type **struct MsgBuf** as above and use it for the buffer, receiving until enough bytes have been returned.

```
struct MsgBuf msg;
void *buffer = (void *) &msg;
int rBytes, rv;
   .
   .
   .
for (rBytes = 0; rBytes < sizeof(msg); rBytes += rv)
{
  if ((rv = recv(s, buffer+rBytes,
                  sizeof(msg)-rBytes, 0)) <= 0)... /* handle error */
}
/* byte order! */
msg.centsDeposited = ntohl(msg.centsDeposited);
   .
   .
   .
```

With text-string representations, the approach we first used is typical: A particular character (in our case, the space character) or sequence of characters delimits fields, and a message is made up of a known number of fields. Receiving messages that are framed by unique markers—as in the ASCII-string version of our bank example, where the end of the message is indicated by the second space character—is not quite trivial with TCP sockets, because message boundaries are not preserved. In particular, if one side can send two messages back-to-back, there is a possibility that the data returned in a single recv() call at the receiver may span the boundary between the two messages. (The subtleties of the relationship between sends and receives are discussed in more detail in Section 6.1.) For this reason it is usually necessary to implement some kind of parse-as-you-receive code when using TCP sockets with text-delimited messages.

For our original two-number bank example, we could write a routine, ReceiveMessage(), which parses the message as it is received. Its specification is that it *only* returns after a complete message, whose length does not exceed a given limit, has been (received and) copied into a given buffer; otherwise, it calls one of the error-exit routines. The value returned is the length of the message copied into the buffer.

```
#define DELIMCHAR ' '
#define FIELDSPERMSG 2

int ReceiveMessage(int s, char *buf, int maxLen)
{
  int received=0;
  int delimCount=0;
  int rv;
```

```
    while ((received < maxLen) && (delimCount < FIELDSPERMSG))
    {
      rv = recv(buf+received, 1, 0);
      if (rv < 0)
        DieWithError("recv() failed");
      else if (rv == 0)
        DieWithError("unexpected end of transmission");
      if (*(buf+received) == DELIMCHAR) /* count delimiters */
        delimCount += 1;
      received += 1;
    }
    return received;
}
```

Notice that ReceiveMessage() only asks for one byte at a time; if it did not, recv() might return the second space character in the first byte and one or more bytes of the next message right after it. Although it is less efficient to receive characters one at a time, receiving in bigger chunks requires maintaining state (about messages partially received) across calls to ReceiveMessage(); we have opted here for simplicity.

You can no doubt imagine various functional enhancements to ReceiveMessage(). For example, you might replace the delimiters with null characters so that the calling program can treat the field contents as strings. You might also check that the fields are properly formed, that is, consist of a single sign followed by nothing but decimal digits. You might even perform the conversion from string to native representation.

In the limit of such enhancements, the ReceiveMessage() routine becomes a general *presentation service*, which handles all responsibility for details of message encoding. The presentation service is typically provided with a grammar describing the allowable message formats of the application protocol; this can be done offline. The grammar is compiled into a parser, which reads bytes from the socket and returns pointers to fully converted and validated C structures.

Various standards exist for such presentation services. These are capable of encoding arbitrarily complex data structures such as nested records, arrays, and floating-point numbers in a machine-independent way [17, 7, 14]. Such protocols are used in application protocols such as Network File System (NFS) [18, 19], Remote Procedure Call (RPC) [10], and the Simple Network Management Protocol (SNMP) [1].

Thought Questions

1. What is the biggest number that can be stored as an unsigned integer on your machine?

2. Does it make any difference whether a variable that will store a port number is declared **signed** or **unsigned**? How?

Using UDP Sockets

The User Datagram Protocol (UDP) provides an end-to-end service different from that of TCP. In fact, UDP performs only two functions: (1) It adds another layer of addressing (ports) to that of IP, and (2) it detects data corruption that may occur in transit and discards any corrupted datagrams. Because of this simplicity, UDP (datagram) sockets have some different characteristics from the TCP (stream) sockets we saw earlier.

For example, UDP sockets do not have to be connected before being used. Where TCP is analogous to telephone communication, UDP is analogous to communicating by mail: You do not have to "connect" before you send a package or letter, but you do have to specify the destination address for each one. In receiving, a UDP socket is like a mailbox into which letters or packages from many different sources can be placed.

As soon as it is created, a UDP socket can be used to send/receive messages to/from any address and to/from many *different* addresses in succession. To allow the destination address to be specified for each message, the sockets API provides a different sending routine that is generally used with UDP sockets: sendto(). Similarly, the recvfrom() routine returns the source address of each received message in addition to the message itself.

---

int sendto(**int** *socket*, **const void** **msg*, **unsigned int** *msgLength*, **int** *flags*,
         struct sockaddr **destAddr*, **unsigned int** *addrLen*)
int recvfrom(**int** *socket*, **void** **msg*, **unsigned int** *msgLength*, **int** *flags*,
         struct sockaddr **srcAddr*, **unsigned int** **addrLen*)

The first four parameters to sendto() are the same as those for send(). The two additional parameters specify the message's destination. Again, they will invariably be a pointer to a **struct sockaddr_in** and sizeof(struct sockaddr_in), respectively. Similarly, recvfrom() takes the same parameters as recv() but, in addition, has two parameters that inform the caller of the source of the received datagram. One thing to note is that *addrLen* is an *in-out* parameter in recvfrom(): On input it specifies the size of the address buffer *srcAddr*; on output it specifies the size of the address that was copied into the buffer. Two errors often made by novices are (1) passing an integer value instead of a pointer to an integer for *addrLen* and (2) forgetting to initialize the pointed-to length variable to contain sizeof(struct sockaddr_in).

Another difference between UDP sockets and TCP sockets is the way they deal with message boundaries: UDP sockets preserve them. This makes receiving an application message simpler, in some ways, than with TCP sockets. We will discuss this further in Section 4.3. A final difference is that the end-to-end transport service UDP provides is best effort: There is no guarantee that a message sent via a UDP socket will arrive at its destination. This means that a program using UDP sockets must be prepared to deal with loss and reordering of messages. (We'll see an example of that later.) First, we introduce the API calls relevant to UDP sockets through simple client and server programs. As before, they implement a trivial echo protocol.

4.1   UDP Client

Our UDP echo client, UDPEchoClient.c, looks similar to TCPEchoClient.c (page 13), except that it does not call connect(), and it only needs to do a single receive, because UDP sockets preserve message boundaries, unlike TCP's byte-stream service. Of course, a UDP client only communicates with a UDP server. Many systems include a UDP echo server for debugging and testing purposes; the server simply echoes whatever messages it receives back to wherever they came from. Our echo client performs the following steps: (1) it sends the echo string to the server, (2) it receives the echo, and (3) it shuts down the program.

UDPEchoClient.c

```
 0  #include <stdio.h>       /* for printf() and fprintf() */
 1  #include <sys/socket.h>  /* for socket(), connect(), sendto(), and recvfrom() */
 2  #include <arpa/inet.h>   /* for sockaddr_in and inet_addr() */
 3  #include <stdlib.h>      /* for atoi() */
 4  #include <string.h>      /* for memset() */
 5  #include <unistd.h>      /* for close() */
 6
 7  #define ECHOMAX 255      /* Longest string to echo */
 8
 9  void DieWithError(char *errorMessage);  /* External error handling function */
10
11  int main(int argc, char *argv[])
12  {
13      int sock;                        /* Socket descriptor */
14      struct sockaddr_in echoServAddr; /* Echo server address */
15      struct sockaddr_in fromAddr;     /* Source address of echo */
```

```
16      unsigned short echoServPort;    /* Echo server port */
17      unsigned int fromSize;          /* In-out of address size for recvfrom() */
18      char *servIP;                   /* IP address of server */
19      char *echoString;               /* String to send to echo server */
20      char echoBuffer[ECHOMAX+1];     /* Buffer for receiving echoed string */
21      int echoStringLen;              /* Length of string to echo */
22      int respStringLen;              /* Length of received response */
23
24      if ((argc < 3) || (argc > 4))    /* Test for correct number of arguments */
25      {
26          fprintf(stderr,"Usage: %s <Server IP> <Echo Word> [<Echo Port>]\n", argv[0]);
27          exit(1);
28      }
29
30      servIP = argv[1];           /* First arg: server IP address (dotted quad)*/
31      echoString = argv[2];       /* Second arg: string to echo */
32
33      if ((echoStringLen = strlen(echoString)) > ECHOMAX)  /* Check input length */
34          DieWithError("Echo word too long");
35
36      if (argc == 4)
37          echoServPort = atoi(argv[3]);  /* Use given port, if any */
38      else
39          echoServPort = 7;  /* 7 is the well-known port for the echo service */
40
41      /* Create a datagram/UDP socket */
42      if ((sock = socket(PF_INET, SOCK_DGRAM, IPPROTO_UDP)) < 0)
43          DieWithError("socket() failed");
44
45      /* Construct the server address structure */
46      memset(&echoServAddr, 0, sizeof(echoServAddr));     /* Zero out structure */
47      echoServAddr.sin_family = AF_INET;                  /* Internet addr family */
48      echoServAddr.sin_addr.s_addr = inet_addr(servIP);   /* Server IP address */
49      echoServAddr.sin_port   = htons(echoServPort);      /* Server port */
50
51      /* Send the string to the server */
52      if (sendto(sock, echoString, echoStringLen, 0, (struct sockaddr *)
53              &echoServAddr, sizeof(echoServAddr)) != echoStringLen)
54          DieWithError("sendto() sent a different number of bytes than expected");
55
56      /* Recv a response */
57      fromSize = sizeof(fromAddr);
58      if ((respStringLen = recvfrom(sock, echoBuffer, ECHOMAX, 0,
59          (struct sockaddr *) &fromAddr, &fromSize)) != echoStringLen)
60          DieWithError("recvfrom() failed");
```

```
61
62    if (echoServAddr.sin_addr.s_addr != fromAddr.sin_addr.s_addr)
63    {
64        fprintf(stderr,"Error: received a packet from unknown source.\n");
65        exit(1);
66    }
67
68    /* null-terminate the received data */
69    echoBuffer[respStringLen] = '\0';
70    printf("Received: %s\n", echoBuffer);    /* Print the echoed arg */
71
72    close(sock);
73    exit(0);
74  }
```

UDPEchoClient.c

1. **Program setup and parameter parsing:** lines 0–39

2. **Socket creation and setup:** lines 42–43
   This is almost identical to the TCP echo client, except that we create a datagram (SOCK_DGRAM) socket using UDP (IPPROTO_UDP). Note that we do not need to connect() before communicating with the server.

3. **Send a single echo datagram:** lines 46–54
   With UDP we simply tell sendto() the datagram destination in *echoServAddr*. We could change this destination for every call to sendto(). The first call to sendto() also assigns an arbitrarily chosen port number, not in use by any other socket, to the socket identified by *sock*, because we have not bound the socket to a port number. We do not know (or care) what the chosen port number is, but the server will use it to send the echoed message back to us.

4. **Get and print echo reply:** lines 57–70

   ■ **Receive a message:** lines 57–60
   We initialize *fromSize* to contain the size of the address buffer (*fromAddr*) and then pass its address as the last parameter. recvfrom() blocks until a UDP datagram addressed to this socket's port arrives. It then copies the data from the first arriving datagram into *echoBuffer* and copies the Internet address and (UDP) port number of its source from the packet's headers into the structure *fromAddr*. Note that the data buffer is actually one byte bigger than ECHOMAX, to allow us to add a null byte to terminate the string.

   ■ **Check message source:** lines 62–66
   Because there is no connection, a received message can come from any source. The output parameter *fromAddr* informs us of the datagram's source, and we check it to

make sure it matches the server's Internet address. Although it is very unlikely that a packet would ever arrive from any other source, we include this check to emphasize that it is possible. To be completely careful, we should check the port as well.

■ **Print received string:** lines 69-70
Before printing the received data as a string, we first ensure that it is null-terminated.

5. **Wrap up:** lines 72-73

This example client is fine as an introduction to the UDP socket calls; it will work correctly most of the time. However, it would not be suitable for production use, because if a message is lost going to or from the server, the call to recvfrom() blocks forever, and the program does not terminate. Clients generally deal with this problem through the use of *timeouts*, a subject we cover in Section 5.3.3.

4.2 UDP Server

Our next example program implements the UDP version of the echo server, UDPEchoServer.c. The server is very simple: It loops forever, receiving a message and then sending the same message back to wherever it came from. Actually, the server only receives and sends back the first 255 characters of the message; any excess is silently discarded by the sockets implementation. (See Section 4.3 for an explanation.)

UDPEchoServer.c

```
0   #include <stdio.h>       /* for printf() and fprintf() */
1   #include <sys/socket.h>  /* for socket() and bind() */
2   #include <arpa/inet.h>   /* for sockaddr_in and inet_ntoa() */
3   #include <stdlib.h>      /* for atoi() */
4   #include <string.h>      /* for memset() */
5   #include <unistd.h>      /* for close() */
6
7   #define ECHOMAX 255      /* Longest string to echo */
8
9   void DieWithError(char *errorMessage);  /* External error handling function */
10
11  int main(int argc, char *argv[])
12  {
13      int sock;                       /* Socket */
14      struct sockaddr_in echoServAddr; /* Local address */
15      struct sockaddr_in echoClntAddr; /* Client address */
16      unsigned int cliAddrLen;         /* Length of incoming message */
17      char echoBuffer[ECHOMAX];        /* Buffer for echo string */
18      unsigned short echoServPort;     /* Server port */
19      int recvMsgSize;                 /* Size of received message */
```

```
20
21       if (argc != 2)            /* Test for correct number of parameters */
22       {
23           fprintf(stderr,"Usage:  %s <UDP SERVER PORT>\n", argv[0]);
24           exit(1);
25       }
26
27       echoServPort = atoi(argv[1]);  /* First arg: local port */
28
29       /* Create socket for sending/receiving datagrams */
30       if ((sock = socket(PF_INET, SOCK_DGRAM, IPPROTO_UDP)) < 0)
31           DieWithError("socket() failed");
32
33       /* Construct local address structure */
34       memset(&echoServAddr, 0, sizeof(echoServAddr));   /* Zero out structure */
35       echoServAddr.sin_family = AF_INET;                /* Internet address family */
36       echoServAddr.sin_addr.s_addr = htonl(INADDR_ANY); /* Any incoming interface */
37       echoServAddr.sin_port = htons(echoServPort);      /* Local port */
38
39       /* Bind to the local address */
40       if (bind(sock, (struct sockaddr *) &echoServAddr, sizeof(echoServAddr)) < 0)
41           DieWithError("bind() failed");
42
43       for (;;) /* Run forever */
44       {
45           /* Set the size of the in-out parameter */
46           cliAddrLen = sizeof(echoClntAddr);
47
48           /* Block until receive message from a client */
49           if ((recvMsgSize = recvfrom(sock, echoBuffer, ECHOMAX, 0,
50               (struct sockaddr *) &echoClntAddr, &cliAddrLen)) < 0)
51               DieWithError("recvfrom() failed");
52
53           printf("Handling client %s\n", inet_ntoa(echoClntAddr.sin_addr));
54
55           /* Send received datagram back to the client */
56           if (sendto(sock, echoBuffer, recvMsgSize, 0,
57               (struct sockaddr *) &echoClntAddr, sizeof(echoClntAddr)) != recvMsgSize)
58               DieWithError("sendto() sent a different number of bytes than expected");
59       }
60       /* NOT REACHED */
61   }
```

UDPEchoServer.c

1. **Program setup and parameter parsing:** lines 0-27

2. **Socket creation and setup:** lines 30-41
   This is nearly identical to the TCP echo server, except that we create a datagram (SOCK_DGRAM) socket using UDP (IPPROTO_UDP). Also, we do not need to call listen() because there is no connection setup—the socket is ready to receive messages as soon as it has an address.

3. **Iteratively handle incoming echo requests:** lines 43-59
   Several key differences between UDP and TCP servers are demonstrated in how each communicates with the client. In the TCP server, we blocked on a call to accept() awaiting a connection from a client. Since UDP servers do not establish a connection, we do not need to get a new socket for each client. Instead, we can immediately call recvfrom() with the same socket that was bound to the desired port number.

   - **Receive an echo request:** lines 46-51
     recvfrom() blocks until a datagram is received from a client. Since there is no connection, each datagram may come from a different sender, and we learn the source at the same time we receive the datagram. recvfrom() puts the address of the source in *echoClntAddr*. The length of this address buffer is specified by *cliAddrLen*. Notice that the UDP server uses a single socket for all communication, unlike the TCP server, which uses accept() to get a new socket for each client.

   - **Send echo reply:** lines 56-58
     sendto() transmits the data in *echoBuffer* back to the address specified by *echoClntAddr*. Each received datagram is considered a single client echo request, so we only need a single send and receive—unlike the TCP echo server, where we needed to receive until the client closed the connection.

4.3 Sending and Receiving with UDP Sockets

A subtle but important difference between TCP and UDP is that *UDP preserves message boundaries*. In particular, each call to recvfrom() returns data from at most one sendto() call. Moreover, different calls to recvfrom() will never return data from the same call to sendto() (unless you use the MSG_PEEK flag with recvfrom()—see next page).

When a call to send() on a TCP socket returns, all the caller knows is that the data has been copied into a buffer for transmission; the data may or may not have actually been transmitted yet. (This is explained in more detail in Chapter 6.) However, UDP does not buffer data for possible retransmission because it does not recover from errors. This means that by the time a call to sendto() on a UDP socket returns, the message has been passed to the underlying channel for transmission and is (or soon will be) on its way out the door.

Between the time a message arrives from the network and the time its data is returned via recv() or recvfrom(), the data is stored in a first-in, first-out (FIFO) receive buffer. With a connected TCP socket, all received-but-not-yet-delivered bytes are treated as one continuous sequence (Chapter 6, Section 6.1). For a UDP socket, however, the bytes from different messages may have come from different senders. Therefore, the boundaries between them need to be preserved so that the data from each message can be returned with the proper address. The buffer really contains a FIFO sequence of "chunks" of data, each with an associated source address. A call to recvfrom() will never return more than one of these chunks. However, if recvfrom() is called with size parameter n, and the size of the first chunk in the receive FIFO is bigger than n, only the first n bytes of the chunk are returned. *The remaining bytes are quietly discarded, with no indication to the receiving program.*

For this reason, a receiver should always supply a buffer big enough to hold the largest message allowed by its application protocol at the time it calls recvfrom(). This technique will guarantee that no data will be lost. The maximum amount of data that can ever be returned by recvfrom() on a UDP socket is 65,507 bytes—the largest payload that can be carried in a UDP datagram.

Alternatively, the receiver can use the MSG_PEEK flag with recvfrom() to "peek" at the first chunk waiting to be received. This flag causes the received data to remain in the socket's receive FIFO so it can be received more than once. This strategy can be useful if memory is scarce, application messages vary widely in size, and each message carries information about its size in the first few bytes. The receiver first calls recvfrom() with MSG_PEEK and a small buffer, examines the first few bytes of the message to determine its size, and then calls recvfrom() again (without MSG_PEEK) with a buffer big enough to hold the entire message. In the usual case where memory is not scarce, using a buffer big enough for the largest possible message is simpler.

Thought Questions

1. Verify experimentally the size of the largest datagram you can send and receive using a UDP socket.

2. While UDPEchoServer.c explicitly specifies its local port number using bind(), we do not call bind() in UDPEchoClient.c. How is the UDP echo client's socket given a port number? (Answer is different for UDP.)

chapter **5**

Socket Programming

Our client and server examples demonstrate the basic model for socket programming. The next step is to integrate these ideas into various programming models such as multitasking, signalling, and broadcasting. We demonstrate these principles in the context of standard UNIX programming; however, most modern operating systems support similar features (e.g., processes and threads).

5.1 Socket Options

The TCP/IP protocol developers spent a good deal of time thinking about the default behaviors that would satisfy most applications. (If you doubt this, read RFCs 1122 and 1123, which describe in excruciating detail the recommended behaviors—based on years of experience—for implementations of the TCP/IP protocols.) For most applications, the designers did a good job; however, it is seldom the case that "one-size-fits-all" really fits all. For example, each socket has an associated receive buffer (Section 6.1). How big should it be? Each implementation has a default size; however, this value may not always be appropriate for your application. This particular aspect of a socket's behavior, along with many others, is associated with a *socket option*: You can change the receive buffer size of a socket by modifying the value of the associated socket option. The functions getsockopt() and setsockopt() allow socket option values to be queried and set, respectively. For both functions, *socket* must be a socket descriptor allocated by socket().

---

int getsockopt(**int** *socket*, **int** *level*, **int** *optName*, **void** **optVal*, **unsigned int** **optLen*)
int setsockopt(**int** *socket*, **int** *level*, **int** *optName*, **const void** **optVal*, **unsigned int** *optLen*)

The available socket options are divided into levels that correspond to the layers of the protocol stack; the second parameter indicates the level of the option in question. Some options are protocol independent and are thus handled by the socket layer itself (SOL_SOCKET), some are specific to the transport protocol (IPPROTO_TCP), and some are handled by the internetwork protocol (IPPROTO_IP). The option itself is specified by the integer *optName*. The parameter *optVal* is a pointer to a buffer. For getsockopt(), the option's current value is placed in that buffer, whereas for setsockopt(), the socket option is set to the value in the buffer. In both calls, *optLen* specifies the length of the buffer, which must be correct for the particular option in question. Note that in getsockopt(), *optLen* is an in-out parameter, initially pointing to an integer containing the size of the buffer; on return the pointed-to integer contains the size of the option value. The following code segment demonstrates how to fetch and then double the current number of bytes in the socket's receive buffer:

```
int rcvBufferSize;
int sockOptSize;
.
.
.
/* Retrieve and print the default buffer size */
sockOptSize = sizeof(rcvBufferSize);
if (getsockopt(sock, SOL_SOCKET, SO_RCVBUF, &rcvBufferSize, &sockOptSize) < 0)
    DieWithError("getsockopt() failed");
printf("Initial Receive Buffer Size: %d\n", rcvBufferSize);

/* Double the buffer size */
rcvBufferSize *= 2;
if (setsockopt(sock, SOL_SOCKET, SO_RCVBUF, &rcvBufferSize, sizeof(rcvBufferSize)) < 0)
    DieWithError("setsockopt() failed");
```

Table 5.1 shows some commonly used options at each level, including a description and the data type of the buffer pointed to by *optVal*.

5.2 Signals

Signals provide a mechanism for notifying programs that certain events have occurred—for example, the user typed the "interrupt" character, or a timer expired. Some of the events (and therefore the notification) may occur *asynchronously*, which means that the notification is delivered to the program regardless of where in the code it is executing. When a signal is delivered to a running program, one of four things happens:

1. The signal is ignored. The process is never aware that the signal was delivered.

2. The program is forcibly terminated by the operating system.

3. A *signal-handling routine*, specified by (and part of) the program, is executed. This execution happens in a different thread of control from the main thread(s) of the program so that the program is not necessarily immediately aware of it.

optName	Type	Values	Description
SOL_SOCKET Level			
SO_BROADCAST	**int**	0,1	Broadcast allowed
SO_KEEPALIVE	**int**	0,1	Keepalive messages enabled (if implemented by the protocol)
SO_LINGER	**linger**{}	time	Time to delay close() return waiting for confirmation (see Section 6.4.2)
SO_RCVBUF	**int**	bytes	Bytes in the socket receive buffer (see code on page 44 and Section 6.1)
SO_RCVLOWAT	**int**	bytes	Minimum number of available bytes that will cause recv() to return
SO_REUSEADDR	**int**	0,1	Binding allowed (under certain conditions) to an address or port already in use (see Section 6.4 and 6.5)
SO_SNDLOWAT	**int**	bytes	Minimum bytes to send
SO_SNDBUF	**int**	bytes	Bytes in the socket send buffer (see Section 6.1)
IPPROTO_TCP Level			
TCP_MAX	**int**	seconds	Seconds between keepalive messages.
TCP_NODELAY	**int**	0,1	Disallow delay for data merging (Nagle's algorithm)
IPPROTO_IP Level			
IP_TTL	**int**	0-255	Time-to-live for unicast IP packets
IP_MULTICAST_TTL	**unsigned char**	0-255	Time-to-live for multicast IP packets (see MulticastSender.c on page 81)
IP_MULTICAST_LOOP	**int**	0,1	Enables multicast socket to receive packets it sent
IP_ADD_MEMBERSHIP	**ip_mreq**{}	group address	Enables reception of packets addressed to the specified multicast group (see MulticastReceiver.c on page 83)—set only
IP_DROP_MEMBERSHIP	**ip_mreq**{}	group address	Disables reception of packets addressed to the specified multicast group—set only

Table 5.1: Socket Options

4. The signal is *blocked*, that is, prevented from having any effect until the program takes action to allow its delivery. Each process has a *mask*, indicating which signals are currently blocked in that process. (Actually, each thread in a program can have its own signal mask.)

UNIX has dozens of different signals, each indicating the occurrence of a different type of event. Each signal has a system-defined *default behavior*, which is one of the first two possibilities listed above. For example, termination is the default behavior for SIGINT, which is delivered when the interrupt character (usually Control-C) is received via the controlling terminal for that process.

Signals are a complicated animal, and a full treatment is beyond the scope of this book. However, some signals are frequently encountered in the context of socket programming. Moreover, any program that sends on a TCP socket must explicitly deal with at least one of them (SIGPIPE) in order to be robust. Therefore, we present the basics of dealing with signals, focusing on these five:

Signal	Triggering Event	Default Behavior
SIGALRM	Expiration of an alarm timer	Termination
SIGCHLD	Child process exit	Ignore
SIGINT	Interrupt char (Control-C) input	Termination
SIGIO	Socket ready for I/O	Ignore
SIGPIPE	Attempt to write to a closed socket	Termination

An application program can change the default behavior[1] for a particular signal using sigaction():

---

int sigaction(**int** *whichSignal*, **const struct sigaction** **newAction*, **struct sigaction** **oldAction*)

---

sigaction() returns 0 on success and −1 on failure; details of its semantics, however, are a bit more involved.

Each signal is identified by an integer constant; *whichSignal* specifies the signal for which the behavior is being changed. The *newAction* parameter points to a **sigaction** structure that defines the new behavior for the given signal type; if the pointer *oldAction* is non-null, a **sigaction** structure describing the previous behavior for the given signal is copied into it, as shown here:

---

[1] For some signals, the default behavior cannot be changed nor can the signal be blocked; however, this is not true for any of the five we consider.

```
struct sigaction {
    void (*sa_handler)(int);    /* Signal handler */
    sigset_t sa_mask;           /* Signals to be blocked during handler execution */
    int sa_flags;               /* Flags to modify default behavior */
};
```

The field sa_handler (of type "pointer to function with a single, integer parameter that returns void") controls which of the first three possibilities occurs when a signal is delivered (i.e., when it is not masked). If its value is the special constant SIG_IGN, the signal will be ignored. If its value is SIG_DFL, the default behavior for that signal will be used. If its value is the address of a function (which is guaranteed to be different from the two constants), that function will be invoked with a parameter indicating the signal that was delivered. (If the same handler function is used for multiple signals, the parameter can be used to determine which one caused the invocation.)

Signals can be "nested" in the following sense: While one signal is being handled, another is delivered. As you can imagine, this can get rather complicated. Fortunately, the sigaction() mechanism allows some signals to be temporarily blocked (in addition to those that are already blocked by the process's signal mask) while the specified signal is handled. The field sa_mask specifies the signals to be blocked while handling *whichSignal*; it is only meaningful when sa_handler is not SIG_IGN or SIG_DFL. By default *whichSignal* is always blocked regardless of whether it is reflected in sa_mask. (On some systems, setting the flag SA_NODEFER in sa_flags allows the specified signal to be delivered while it is being handled.) The sa_flags field controls some further details of the way *whichSignal* is handled; these details are beyond the scope of this discussion.

sa_mask is implemented as a set of boolean flags, one for each type of signal. This set of flags can be manipulated with the following four functions:

---

int sigemptyset(**sigset_t** **set*)
int sigfillset(**sigset_t** **set*)
int sigaddset(**sigset_t** **set*, **int** *whichSignal*)
int sigdelset(**sigset_t** **set*, **int** *whichSignal*)

---

sigfillset() and sigemptyset() set and unset all of the flags in the given set. sigaddset() and sigdelset() set and unset individual flags, specified by the signal number, in the given set. All four functions return 0 for success and −1 for failure.

SigAction.c shows a simple sigaction() example to provide a handler for SIGINT by setting up a signal handler and then entering an infinite loop. When the program receives an interrupt signal, the handler function, specified by sigaction(), executes and exits the program.

SigAction.c

```
0   #include <stdio.h>  /* for printf() */
1   #include <signal.h> /* for sigaction() */
2   #include <unistd.h> /* for pause() */
3
4   void DieWithError(char *errorMessage);       /* Error handling function */
5   void InterruptSignalHandler(int signalType); /* Interrupt signal handling function*/
6
7   int main(int argc, char *argv[])
8   {
9       struct sigaction handler;    /* Signal handler specification structure */
10
11      /* Set InterruptSignalHandler() as handler function */
12      handler.sa_handler =  InterruptSignalHandler;
13      /* Create mask that masks all signals */
14      if (sigfillset(&handler.sa_mask) < 0)
15          DieWithError("sigfillset() failed");
16      /* No flags */
17      handler.sa_flags = 0;
18
19      /* Set signal handling for interrupt signals */
20      if (sigaction(SIGINT, &handler, 0) < 0)
21          DieWithError("sigaction() failed");
22
23      for(;;)
24          pause();  /* suspend program until signal received */
25
26      exit(0);
27  }
28
29  void InterruptSignalHandler(int signalType)
30  {
31      printf("Interrupt Received.  Exiting program.\n");
32      exit(1);
33  }
```

---

1. **Signal handler function prototype:** line 5
2. **Set up signal handler:** lines 9–21
   - **Assign function to handle signal:** line 12
   - **Fill signal mask:** lines 14–15

■ **Set signal handler for SIGINT:** lines 20-21

3. **Loop forever until SIGINT:** lines 23-24
   pause() suspends the process until a signal is received.

4. **Function to handle signal:** lines 29-33
   InterruptSignalHandler() prints a message and exits the program.

So what happens when a signal that would otherwise be delivered is blocked, say, because another signal is being handled? Delivery is postponed until the handler completes. Such a signal is said to be *pending*. It is important to realize that signals are *not* queued— a signal is either pending or it is not. If the same signal is delivered more than once while it is being handled, the handler is only executed once more after it completes the original execution. Consider the case where three SIGINT signals arrive while the signal handler for SIGINT is already executing. The first of the three SIGINT signals is blocked; however, the subsequent two signals are lost. When the SIGINT signal handler function completes, the system executes the handler only *once* again. We must be prepared to handle this behavior in our applications. To see this in action, modify InterruptSignalHandler() in SigAction.c as follows:

```
void InterruptSignalHandler(int ignored)
{
        printf("Interrupt Received.\n");
        sleep(3);
}
```

The signal handler for SIGINT sleeps for three seconds and returns, instead of exiting. Now when you execute the program, hit the interrupt key (Control-C) several times in succession. If you hit the interrupt key more than two times in a row, you still only see two "Interrupt Received" messages. The first interrupt signal invokes InterruptSignalHandler(), which sleeps for three seconds. The second interrupt is blocked because SIGINT is already being handled. The third and fourth interrupts are lost. Be warned that you will no longer be able to stop your program with a keyboard interrupt. You will need to explicitly send another signal (such as SIGTERM) to the process using the **kill** command.

One of the most important aspect of signals relates to the sockets interface. If a signal is delivered while the program is blocked in a socket call (such as a recv() or connect()), and a handler for that signal has been specified, as soon as the handler completes, the socket call will return −1 with errno set to EINTR. Thus, your programs that catch and handle signals need to be prepared for these erroneous returns from those calls.

Later in this chapter we encounter the first four signals mentioned above. Here we briefly describe the semantics of SIGPIPE. Consider the following scenario: A server (or client) has a connected TCP socket, and the other end unexpectedly closes the connection, say, because the program crashed. How does the server find out that the connection is broken? The answer is that it doesn't, until it tries to send on the socket. At that point, SIGPIPE is delivered. (Thus, SIGPIPE is delivered *synchronously* and not asynchronously.) This fact is especially significant for servers, because the default behavior for SIGPIPE is to terminate the program. Thus, servers that don't change this behavior can be terminated by misbehaving clients. Servers should always handle SIGPIPE so that they can detect the client's disappearance and reclaim any resources that were in use to service it.

5.3 Nonblocking I/O

The default behavior of a socket call is to block until the requested action is completed. For example, the recv() function in TCPEchoClient.c (page 13) does not return until at least one message from the echo server is received. Of course, a process with a blocked function is suspended by the operating system.

A socket call may block for several reasons. Data reception functions (recv() and recvfrom()) block if data is not available. A send() on a TCP socket may block if there is not sufficient space to buffer the transmitted data (see Section 6.1). Connection-related functions for TCP sockets block until a connection has been established. For example, accept() in TCPEchoServer.c (page 19) blocks until a client establishes a connection with connect(). Long round-trip times, high error rate connections, or a slow (or deceased) server may cause a call to connect() to block for a significant amount of time. In all of these cases, the function returns only after the request has been satisfied.

What about a program that has other tasks to perform while waiting for call completion (e.g., update the "busy" cursor or respond to user requests)? These programs may have no time to wait on a blocked system call. What about lost UDP datagrams? In UDPEchoClient.c (page 36), the client sends a datagram to the server and then waits to receive a response. If either the datagram sent from the client or the echoed datagram from the server is lost, our echo client blocks indefinitely. In this case, we need recvfrom() to unblock after some amount of time to allow the client to handle the datagram loss. Fortunately, several mechanisms are available for controlling unwanted blocking behaviors. We deal with three here: nonblocking sockets, asynchronous I/O, and timeouts.

5.3.1 Nonblocking Sockets

One obvious solution to the problem of undesirable blocking is to change the behavior of the socket so that all calls are *nonblocking*. For such a socket, if a requested operation can be completed immediately, the call's return value indicates success; otherwise it indicates failure (usually −1). In either case the call does not block indefinitely. In the case of failure, we need the ability to distinguish between failure due to blocking and other types of failures. If the failure occurred because the call would have blocked, the system sets errno to EWOULDBLOCK,[2] except for connect(), which returns an errno of EINPROGRESS.

---

[2] Some sockets implementations return EAGAIN. However, on many systems, EAGAIN and EWOULDBLOCK are the same error number.

We can change the default blocking behavior with a call to fcntl() ("file control").

---

int fcntl(int *socket*, int *command*, long *argument*)

As the name suggests, this call can be used with any kind of file: *socket* must be a valid file (or socket) descriptor. The operation to be performed is given by *command*. The behavior we want to modify is controlled by flags (not the same as socket options) associated with the descriptor, which we can get and set with the F_GETFL and F_SETFL commands. When setting the socket flags, we must specify the new flags in *argument*. The flag that controls nonblocking behavior is O_NONBLOCK. When getting the socket flags, *argument* is 0. We demonstrate the use of a nonblocking socket in the next section in UDPEchoServer-SIGIO.c (page 52) when we describe asynchronous I/O.

There are a few exceptions to this model of nonblocking sockets. For UDP sockets, there are no send buffers, so send() and sendto() never return EWOULDBLOCK. For all but the connect() socket call, the requested operation either completes before returning or none of the operation is performed. For example, recv() either receives data from the socket or returns an error. A nonblocking connect() is different. For UDP, connect() simply assigns a destination address for future data transmissions so it never blocks. For TCP, connect() initiates the TCP connection setup. If the connection cannot be completed without blocking, connect() returns an error, setting errno to EINPROGRESS, indicating that the socket is still working on making the TCP connection. Of course, subsequent data sends and receives cannot happen until the connection is established. Determining when the connection is complete is beyond the scope of this text,[3] so we recommend not setting the socket to nonblocking until after the call to connect().

For eliminating blocking during individual send and receive operations, an alternative is available in some implementations. The *flags* parameter of send(), recv(), sendto(), and recvfrom() allows for modification of some aspects of the behavior on a particular call. Some implementations support the MSG_DONTWAIT flag, which causes nonblocking behavior in any call where it is set in *flags*.

5.3.2 Asynchronous I/O

The difficulty with nonblocking socket calls is that there is no way of knowing when one would succeed, except by periodically trying it until it does (a process known as "polling"). Why not have the operating system inform the program when a socket call will be successful? That way the program can spend its time doing other work until notified that the socket is ready for something to happen. This is called *asynchronous I/O*, and it works by having the SIGIO signal delivered to the process when some I/O-related event occurs on the socket.

---

[3] Well, mostly. Connection completion can be detected using the select() call, described in Section 5.5.

Arranging for SIGIO involves three steps. First, we inform the system of the desired disposition of the signal using sigaction(). Then, we ensure that signals related to the socket will be delivered to *this* process (because multiple processes can have access to the same socket, there might be ambiguity about which should get it) by making it the owner of the socket, using fcntl(). Finally, we mark the socket as being primed for asynchronous I/O by setting a flag (FASYNC), again via fcntl().

In our next example, we adapt UDPEchoServer.c (page 39) to use asynchronous I/O with nonblocking socket calls. The modified server is able to perform other tasks when there are no clients needing an echo. After creating and binding the socket, instead of calling recvfrom() and blocking until a datagram arrives, the asynchronous echo server establishes a signal handler for SIGIO and begins doing other work. When a datagram arrives, the SIGIO signal is delivered to the process, triggering execution of the handler function. The handler function calls recvfrom(), echoes back any received datagrams, and then returns, whereupon the main program continues whatever it was doing. Our description details only the code that differs from the original UDP echo server.

UDPEchoServer-SIGIO.c

```
0   #include <stdio.h>       /* for printf() and fprintf() */
1   #include <sys/socket.h> /* for socket(), bind, and connect() */
2   #include <arpa/inet.h>   /* for sockaddr_in and inet_ntoa() */
3   #include <stdlib.h>      /* for atoi() */
4   #include <string.h>      /* for memset() */
5   #include <unistd.h>      /* for close() */
6   #include <fcntl.h>       /* for fcntl() */
7   #include <sys/file.h>    /* for O_NONBLOCK and FASYNC */
8   #include <signal.h>      /* for signal() and SIGALRM */
9   #include <errno.h>       /* for errno */
10
11  #define ECHOMAX 255      /* Longest string to echo */
12
13  void DieWithError(char *errorMessage);  /* Error handling function */
14  void UseIdleTime();                      /* Function to use idle time */
15  void SIGIOHandler(int signalType);       /* Function to handle SIGIO */
16
17  int sock;                                /* Socket -- GLOBAL for signal handler */
18
19  int main(int argc, char *argv[])
20  {
21      struct sockaddr_in echoServAddr; /* Server address */
22      unsigned short echoServPort;     /* Server port */
23      struct sigaction handler;        /* Signal handling action definition */
24
```

```
25      /* Test for correct number of parameters */
26      if (argc != 2)
27      {
28          fprintf(stderr,"Usage:  %s <SERVER PORT>\n", argv[0]);
29          exit(1);
30      }
31
32      echoServPort = atoi(argv[1]);  /* First arg: local port */
33
34      /* Create socket for sending/receiving datagrams */
35      if ((sock = socket(PF_INET, SOCK_DGRAM, IPPROTO_UDP)) < 0)
36          DieWithError("socket() failed");
37
38      /* Set up the server address structure */
39      memset(&echoServAddr, 0, sizeof(echoServAddr));    /* Zero out structure */
40      echoServAddr.sin_family = AF_INET;                 /* Internet family */
41      echoServAddr.sin_addr.s_addr = htonl(INADDR_ANY);  /* Any incoming interface */
42      echoServAddr.sin_port = htons(echoServPort);       /* Port */
43
44      /* Bind to the local address */
45      if (bind(sock, (struct sockaddr *) &echoServAddr, sizeof(echoServAddr)) < 0)
46          DieWithError("bind() failed");
47
48      /* Set signal handler for SIGIO */
49      handler.sa_handler = SIGIOHandler;
50      /* Create mask that masks all signals */
51      if (sigfillset(&handler.sa_mask) < 0)
52          DieWithError("sigfillset() failed");
53      /* No flags */
54      handler.sa_flags = 0;
55
56      if (sigaction(SIGIO, &handler, 0) < 0)
57          DieWithError("sigaction() failed for SIGIO");
58
59      /* We must own the socket to receive the SIGIO message */
60      if (fcntl(sock, F_SETOWN, getpid()) < 0)
61          DieWithError("Unable to set process owner to us");
62
63      /* Arrange for nonblocking I/O and SIGIO delivery */
64      if (fcntl(sock, F_SETFL, O_NONBLOCK | FASYNC) < 0)
65          DieWithError("Unable to put client sock into nonblocking/async mode");
66
67      /* Go off and do real work; echoing happens in the background */
68
69      for (;;)
70          UseIdleTime();
71
```

```
72       /* NOTREACHED */
73   }
74
75   void UseIdleTime()
76   {
77       printf(".\n");
78       sleep(3);     /* 3 seconds of activity */
79   }
80
81   void SIGIOHandler(int signalType)
82   {
83       struct sockaddr_in echoClntAddr;  /* Address of datagram source */
84       unsigned int clntLen;             /* Address length */
85       int recvMsgSize;                  /* Size of datagram */
86       char echoBuffer[ECHOMAX];         /* Datagram buffer */
87
88       do  /* As long as there is input... */
89       {
90           /* Set the size of the in-out parameter */
91           clntLen = sizeof(echoClntAddr);
92
93           if ((recvMsgSize = recvfrom(sock, echoBuffer, ECHOMAX, 0,
94                   (struct sockaddr *) &echoClntAddr, &clntLen)) < 0)
95           {
96               /* Only acceptable error: recvfrom() would have blocked */
97               if (errno != EWOULDBLOCK)
98                   DieWithError("recvfrom() failed");
99           }
100          else
101          {
102              printf("Handling client %s\n", inet_ntoa(echoClntAddr.sin_addr));
103
104              if (sendto(sock, echoBuffer, recvMsgSize, 0, (struct sockaddr *)
105                  &echoClntAddr, sizeof(echoClntAddr)) != recvMsgSize)
106                  DieWithError("sendto() failed");
107          }
108      } while (recvMsgSize >= 0);
109      /* Nothing left to receive */
110  }
```

UDPEchoServer-SIGIO.c

1. **Additional include files for fcntl() and signals:** lines 6-9

2. **Prototypes for signal and idle time handler:** lines 14-15
   UseIdleTime() implements the other tasks of the UDP echo server. SIGIOHandler() han-

dles SIGIO signals. Note well: UseIdleTime() must be prepared for any "slow" system calls—such as reading from a terminal device—to return −1 as a result of the SIGIO signal being delivered and handled (in which case it should simply verify that errno is EINTR and resume execution).

3. **Echo socket descriptor:** line 17
   We give the echo socket descriptor a global scope so that it can be accessed by the SIGIO handler function.

4. **Set up signal handling:** lines 23, 49–65
   handler is the **sigaction** structure that describes our desired signal-handling behavior. We fill it in, giving the address of the handling routine and the set of signals we want blocked.

   - **Fill in the address of the desired handler:** line 49
   - **Specify signals to be blocked during handling:** lines 51–52
   - **Specify how to handle the SIGIO signal:** lines 56–57
   - **Arrange for SIGIO to go to this process:** lines 60–61
     The F_SETOWN command identifies the process to receive SIGIO for this socket.
   - **Set flags for nonblocking and asynchronous I/O:** lines 64–65
     Finally, we mark the socket (with the FASYNC flag[4]) to indicate that asynchronous I/O is in use, so SIGIO will be delivered on packet arrival. (Everything up to this point was just saying *how* to deal with SIGIO.) Because we do not want SIGIOHandler() to block in recvfrom(), we also set the O_NONBLOCK flag.

5. **Run forever using idle time when available:** lines 69–70

6. **Perform nonechoing server tasks:** lines 75–79

7. **Handle asynchronous I/O:** lines 81–110
   This code is very similar to the loop in our earlier UDPEchoServer.c (page 39). One difference is that here we loop until there are no more pending echo requests to satisfy and then return; this technique enables the main program thread to continue what it was doing.

   - **Receive echo request:** lines 91–98
     The first call to recvfrom() receives the datagram whose arrival prompted the SIGIO signal. Additional datagrams may arrive during execution of the handler, so the do/while loop continues to call recvfrom() until no more datagrams remain to be received. Because *sock* is a nonblocking socket, recvfrom() then returns −1 with errno set to EWOULDBLOCK, terminating the loop and the handler function.
   - **Send echo reply:** lines 104–106
     Just as in the original UDP echo server, sendto() repeats the message back to the client.

---

[4] The name may be different (e.g., O_ASYNC) on some systems.

5.3.3   Timeouts

In the previous subsection, we relied on the system to notify our program of the occurrence of an I/O–related event. Sometimes, however, we may actually need to know that some I/O event has *not* happened for a certain time period. For example, we have mentioned already that UDP messages can be lost; in case of such a loss, our UDP echo client (or any other client that uses UDP, for that matter) will never receive a response to its request. Of course, the client cannot tell directly whether a loss has occurred, so it sets a limit on how long it will wait for a response. For example, the UDP echo client might assume that if the server has not responded to its request within two seconds, the server will never respond. The client's reaction to this three-second *timeout* might be to give up or to try again by resending the request.

The standard method of implementing timeouts is to set an *alarm* before calling a blocking function.

---

unsigned int alarm(unsigned int *secs*)

---

alarm() starts a timer, which expires after the specified number of seconds (*secs*); alarm() returns the number of seconds remaining for any previously scheduled alarm (or 0 if no alarm was scheduled). When the timer expires, a SIGALRM signal is sent to the process, and the handler function for SIGALRM, if any, is executed.

The code we showed earlier in UDPEchoClient.c (page 36) has a problem if either the echo request or response is lost: The client blocks indefinitely on recvfrom(), waiting for a datagram that will never arrive. Our next example program, UDPEchoClient-Timeout.c, modifies the original UDP echo client to retransmit the request message if a response from the echo server is not received within a time limit of two seconds. To implement this, the new client installs a handler for SIGALRM, and just before calling recvfrom(), it sets an alarm for two seconds. At the end of that interval of time, the SIGALRM signal is delivered, and the handler is invoked. When the handler returns, the blocked recvfrom() returns −1 with errno equal to EINTR. The client then resends the echo request to the server. This timeout and retransmission of the echo request happens up to five times before the client gives up and reports failure. Our program description only details the code that differs from the original UDP echo client.

UDPEchoClient-Timeout.c

```
0   #include <stdio.h>       /* for printf() and fprintf() */
1   #include <sys/socket.h>  /* for socket(), connect(), sendto(), and recvfrom() */
2   #include <arpa/inet.h>   /* for sockaddr_in and inet_addr() */
3   #include <stdlib.h>      /* for atoi() */
4   #include <string.h>      /* for memset() */
5   #include <unistd.h>      /* for close() */
6   #include <errno.h>       /* for errno, EINTR */
7   #include <signal.h>      /* for sigaction() */
8
```

```
 9  #define ECHOMAX        255      /* Longest string to echo */
10  #define TIMEOUT_SECS   2        /* Seconds between retransmits */
11  #define MAXTRIES       5        /* Tries before giving up */
12
13  int tries=0;    /* Count of times sent - GLOBAL for signal handler access */
14
15  void DieWithError(char *errorMessage);   /* Error handling function */
16  void CatchAlarm(int ignored);            /* handler for SIGALRM */
17
18  int main(int argc, char *argv[])
19  {
20      int sock;                        /* Socket descriptor */
21      struct sockaddr_in echoServAddr; /* Echo server address */
22      struct sockaddr_in fromAddr;     /* Source address of echo */
23      unsigned short echoServPort;     /* Echo server port */
24      unsigned int fromSize;           /* In-out of address size for recvfrom() */
25      struct sigaction myAction;       /* For setting signal handler */
26      char *servIP;                    /* IP address of server */
27      char *echoString;                /* String to send to echo server */
28      char echoBuffer[ECHOMAX+1];      /* Buffer for echo string */
29      int echoStringLen;               /* Length of string to echo */
30      int respStringLen;               /* Size of received datagram */
31
32      if ((argc < 3) || (argc > 4))    /* Test for correct number of arguments */
33      {
34          fprintf(stderr,"Usage: %s <Server IP> <Echo Word> [<Echo Port>]\n", argv[0]);
35          exit(1);
36      }
37
38      servIP = argv[1];            /* First arg: server IP address (dotted quad) */
39      echoString = argv[2];        /* Second arg: string to echo */
40
41      if ((echoStringLen = strlen(echoString)) > ECHOMAX)
42          DieWithError("Echo word too long");
43
44      if (argc == 4)
45          echoServPort = atoi(argv[3]);  /* Use given port, if any */
46      else
47          echoServPort = 7;  /* 7 is well-known port for echo service */
48
49      /* Create a best-effort datagram socket using UDP */
50      if ((sock = socket(PF_INET, SOCK_DGRAM, IPPROTO_UDP)) < 0)
51          DieWithError("socket() failed");
52
53      /* Set signal handler for alarm signal */
54      myAction.sa_handler = CatchAlarm;
```

```
55          if (sigfillset(&myAction.sa_mask) < 0) /* block everything in handler */
56              DieWithError("sigfillset() failed");
57          myAction.sa_flags = 0;
58
59          if (sigaction(SIGALRM, &myAction, 0) < 0)
60              DieWithError("sigaction() failed for SIGALRM");
61
62          /* Construct the server address structure */
63          memset(&echoServAddr, 0, sizeof(echoServAddr));    /* Zero out structure */
64          echoServAddr.sin_family = AF_INET;
65          echoServAddr.sin_addr.s_addr = inet_addr(servIP);  /* Server IP address */
66          echoServAddr.sin_port = htons(echoServPort);       /* Server port */
67
68          /* Send the string to the server */
69          if (sendto(sock, echoString, echoStringLen, 0, (struct sockaddr *)
70                  &echoServAddr, sizeof(echoServAddr)) != echoStringLen)
71              DieWithError("sendto() sent a different number of bytes than expected");
72
73          /* Get a response  */
74
75          fromSize = sizeof(fromAddr);
76          alarm(TIMEOUT_SECS);           /* Set the timeout */
77          while ((respStringLen = recvfrom(sock, echoBuffer, ECHOMAX, 0,
78              (struct sockaddr *) &fromAddr, &fromSize)) < 0)
79              if (errno == EINTR)     /* Alarm went off  */
80              {
81                  if (tries < MAXTRIES)       /* incremented by signal handler */
82                  {
83                      printf("timed out, %d more tries...\n", MAXTRIES-tries);
84                      if (sendto(sock, echoString, echoStringLen, 0, (struct sockaddr *)
85                              &echoServAddr, sizeof(echoServAddr)) != echoStringLen)
86                          DieWithError("sendto() failed");
87                      alarm(TIMEOUT_SECS);
88                  }
89                  else
90                      DieWithError("No Response");
91              }
92              else
93                  DieWithError("recvfrom() failed");
94
95          /* recvfrom() got something --  cancel the timeout */
96          alarm(0);
97
98          /* null-terminate the received data */
99          echoBuffer[respStringLen] = '\0';
100         printf("Received: %s\n", echoBuffer);    /* Print the received data */
```

```
101
102     close(sock);
103     exit(0);
104  }
105
106  void CatchAlarm(int ignored)      /* handler for SIGALRM */
107  {
108     tries += 1;
109  }
```

UDPEchoClient-Timeout.c

1. **Additional include files for errno and signals:** lines 6-7

2. **Timeout setup:** lines 10-16
   tries is a global variable so that it can be accessed in the signal handler.

3. **Establish signal handler for SIGALRM:** lines 54-60
   This is similar to what we did for SIGIO in `UDPEchoServer-SIGIO.c`.

4. **Set the alarm timer:** line 76
   When/if the alarm timer expires, the handler `CatchAlarm()` will be invoked.

5. **Retransmission loop:** lines 77-93
   We have to loop here because the SIGALRM will cause the `recvfrom()` to return −1. When that happens, we decide whether it was a timeout or not and, if so, retransmit.

   - **Attempt reception:** lines 77-78
   - **Discover the reason for `recvfrom()` failure:** lines 79-93
     If errno equals EINTR, `recvfrom()` returned because it was interrupted by the SIGALRM while waiting for datagram arrival and not because we got a packet. In this case we assume either the echo request or reply is lost. If we have not exceeded the maximum number of retransmission attempts, we retransmit the request to the server; otherwise, we report a failure. After retransmission, we reset the alarm timer to wake us again if the timeout expires.

6. **Handle echo response reception:** lines 96-100

   - **Cancel the alarm timer:** line 96
   - **Ensure that message is null-terminated:** line 99
     `printf()` will output bytes until it encounters '\0', so we need to make sure one is present (otherwise, our program may crash).
   - **Print the received message:** line 100

5.4 Multitasking

Our TCP echo server handles one client at a time. If additional clients connect while one is already being serviced, their connections will be established and they will be able to send their requests, but the server will not echo back their data until it has finished with the first client. This type of socket application is called an *iterative server*. Iterative servers work best for applications where each client requires a small, bounded amount of work by the server; however, if the time required to handle a client can be long, the overall connection time experienced by any waiting clients may become unacceptably long. To demonstrate the problem, add a sleep() after the connect() statement in TCPEchoClient.c (page 13) and experiment with several clients simultaneously accessing the TCP echo server (sleep() simulates an operation that takes significant time such as slow file or network I/O).

Multitasking operating systems, such as UNIX, provide a solution to this dilemma. Using constructs like processes or threads, we can farm out responsibility for each client to an independently executing copy of the server. In this section, we will explore several models of such *concurrent servers*, including per-client processes, per-client threads, and constrained multitasking.

5.4.1 Per-Client Processes

Processes are independently executing programs on the same host. In a per-client process server, for each client connection request we simply create a new process to handle the communication. Processes share the resources of the server host, each servicing its client concurrently.

In UNIX, fork() attempts the creation of a new process, returning −1 on failure. On success, a new process is created that is identical to the calling process, except for its process ID and the return value it receives from fork(). The two processes thereafter execute independently. The process invoking fork() is called the *parent* process, and the newly created process is called the *child*. Since the processes are identical, how do the processes know whether they are parent or child? If the return from fork() is 0, the process knows that it is the child. To the parent, fork() returns the process ID of the new child process.

When a child process terminates, it does not automatically disappear. In UNIX parlance, the child becomes a *zombie*. Zombies consume system resources until they are "harvested" by their parent with a call to waitpid(), as demonstrated in our next example program, TCPEchoServer-Fork.c.

We demonstrate this per-client process, multitasking approach by adapting its use for the TCP echo server. The majority of the program is identical to the original TCPEchoServer.c (page 19). The main difference is that the multitasking server creates a new copy of itself each time it accepts a new connection; each copy handles one client and then terminates. No changes are required to TCPEchoClient.c (page 13) to work with this new server.

We have decomposed this new echo server to improve readability and to allow reuse in our later examples. In addition, we have combined the common subset of include files,

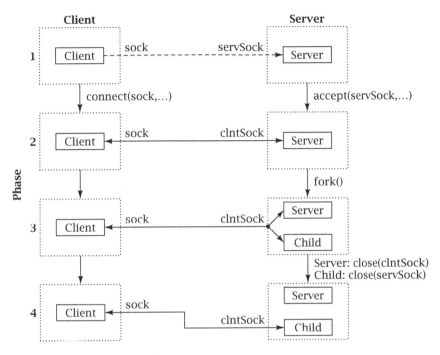

Figure 5.1: Forking TCP echo server.

constants, and prototypes in TCPEchoServer.h (page 64). Our program commentary is limited to differences between the new server and TCPEchoServer.c (page 19).

Figure 5.1 depicts the phases involved in connection setup between the server and a client. The server runs forever, listening for connections on a specified port, and repeatedly (1) accepts an incoming connection from a client and then (2) creates a new process to handle that connection. Note that only the original server process calls fork().

TCPEchoServer-Fork.c

```
0   #include "TCPEchoServer.h"    /* TCP echo server includes */
1   #include <sys/wait.h>         /* for waitpid() */
2
3   int main(int argc, char *argv[])
4   {
5       int servSock;                 /* Socket descriptor for server */
6       int clntSock;                 /* Socket descriptor for client */
7       unsigned short echoServPort;  /* Server port */
8       pid_t processID;              /* Process ID from fork() */
```

```
 9        unsigned int childProcCount = 0; /* Number of child processes */
10
11        if (argc != 2)      /* Test for correct number of arguments */
12        {
13            fprintf(stderr, "Usage:  %s <Server Port>\n", argv[0]);
14            exit(1);
15        }
16
17        echoServPort = atoi(argv[1]);  /* First arg: local port */
18
19        servSock = CreateTCPServerSocket(echoServPort);
20
21        for (;;) /* run forever */
22        {
23            clntSock = AcceptTCPConnection(servSock);
24            /* Fork child process and report any errors */
25            if ((processID = fork()) < 0)
26                DieWithError("fork() failed");
27            else if (processID == 0)  /* This is the child process */
28            {
29                close(servSock);   /* Child closes parent socket */
30                HandleTCPClient(clntSock);
31                close(clntSock);   /* Close child connection socket */
32                exit(0);           /* Child process terminates */
33            }
34
35            printf("with child process: %d\n", (int) processID);
36            close(clntSock);        /* Parent closes child socket descriptor */
37            childProcCount++;       /* Increment number of outstanding child processes */
38
39            while (childProcCount) /* Clean up all zombies */
40            {
41                processID = waitpid((pid_t) -1, NULL, WNOHANG);  /* Nonblocking wait */
42                if (processID < 0)  /* waitpid() error? */
43                    DieWithError("waitpid() failed");
44                else if (processID == 0)  /* No zombie to wait on */
45                    break;
46                else
47                    childProcCount--;  /* Cleaned up after a child */
48            }
49        }
50    /* NOT REACHED */
51 }
```

TCPEchoServer-Fork.c

1. **Additional include file for waitpid():** line 1

2. **Set up to handle multiple processes:** lines 8–9
   childProcCount is a variable to count the number of processes. *processID* holds the process ID returned by fork().

3. **Create server socket:** line 19
   CreateTCPServerSocket() allocates, binds, and marks the server socket as ready to accept incoming connections.

4. **Process dispatch loop:** lines 21–49
   The parent process runs forever, forking a process for each connection request.

   - **Get the next connection:** line 23
     AcceptTCPConnection() blocks until a valid connection is established and returns the socket descriptor for that connection. Connection establishment is depicted in the transition from Phase 1 to 2 in Figure 5.1.

   - **Create a child process to handle the new connection:** lines 25–26
     fork() attempts to duplicate the calling process. If the attempt fails, fork() returns −1. If it succeeds, the child process receives a return value of 0, and the parent receives a return value of the process ID of the child process. When fork() creates a new child process, it copies the socket descriptors from the parent to the child; therefore, after fork(), both the parent and child processes have socket descriptors for the listening socket (*servSock*) and the newly created and connected client socket (*clntSock*), as shown in Phase 3 of Figure 5.1.

   - **Child process execution:** lines 29–31
     The child process is only responsible for dealing with the new client so it can close the listening socket descriptor. However, since the parent process still has a descriptor for the listening socket, this close does not deallocate the socket. This is depicted in the transition from Phase 3 to 4 in Figure 5.1. It is important to note that calling close() only terminates the specified socket if no other processes have a reference to the socket. The child process then executes HandleTCPClient() to handle the connection. After handling the client, the child process calls close() to deallocate the client socket. The child process is terminated with the call to exit().

   - **Parent execution continues:** lines 35–37
     Since the child is handling the new client, the parent can close the socket descriptor of the new connection socket; again, this does not deallocate the socket because the child process also contains a reference.[5] (See the transition from Phase 3 to 4 in

---

[5] Our description of the child and parent execution assumes that the parent executes close() on the client socket before the child. However, it is possible for the client to race ahead and execute the close() call on *clntSock* before the server. In this case, the server's close() performs the actual socket deallocation, but this does not change the behavior of the server from the client's perspective.

Figure 5.1.) The parent keeps a count of the number of outstanding child processes in *childProcCount*.

- **Handle zombies:** lines 39–48

  After each connection request, the parent server process harvests the zombies created by child process termination. The server repeatedly harvests zombies by calling waitpid() until no more of them exist. The first parameter to waitpid() (−1) is a wildcard that instructs it to take any zombie, irrespective of its process ID. The second parameter is a placeholder where waitpid() returns the state of the zombie. Since we do not care about the state, we specify NULL, and no state is returned. Next comes a flag parameter for customizing the behavior of waitpid(). WNOHANG causes it to return immediately if no zombies are found. waitpid() returns one of three value types: failure (returns −1), found zombie (returns pid of zombie), and no zombie (returns 0). If waitpid() found a zombie, we need to decrement *childProcCount* and, if more unharvested children exist (*childProcCount != 0*), look for another zombie. If waitpid() returns without finding a zombie, the parent process breaks out of the zombie harvesting loop.

  There are several other ways to deal with zombies. On some UNIX variants, the default child termination behavior can be changed so that zombie processes are not created (e.g., SA_NOCLDWAIT flag to sigaction()). We do not use this approach because it is not portable. Another approach is to establish a handler function for the SIGCHLD signal. When a child terminates, a SIGCHLD signal is delivered to the process invoking a specified handler function. The handler function uses waitpid() to harvest any zombies. Unfortunately, signals may interrupt at any time, including during blocked system calls (see Section 5.2). The proper method for restarting interrupted system calls differs between UNIX variants. In some systems, restarting is the default behavior. On others, the *sa_flags* field of the **sigaction** structure could be set to SA_RESTART to ensure interrupted system calls restart. On other systems, the interrupted system calls return −1 with errno set to EINTR. In this case, the program must restart the interrupted function. We do not use any of these approaches because they are not portable, and they complicate the program with issues that we are not addressing. We leave it as an exercise for readers to adapt our TCP echo server to use SIGCHLD on their systems.

TCPEchoServer.h

```
0  #include <stdio.h>       /* for printf() and fprintf() */
1  #include <sys/socket.h>  /* for socket(), bind(), and connect() */
2  #include <arpa/inet.h>   /* for sockaddr_in and inet_ntoa() */
3  #include <stdlib.h>       /* for atoi() */
4  #include <string.h>       /* for memset() */
5  #include <unistd.h>       /* for close() */
6
```

```
7    void DieWithError(char *errorMessage);   /* Error handling function */
8    void HandleTCPClient(int clntSocket);    /* TCP client handling function */
9    int CreateTCPServerSocket(unsigned short port); /* Create TCP server socket */
10   int AcceptTCPConnection(int servSock);   /* Accept TCP connection request */
```

TCPEchoServer.h

CreateTCPServerSocket.c

```
0    #include <sys/socket.h> /* for socket(), bind(), and connect() */
1    #include <arpa/inet.h>   /* for sockaddr_in and inet_ntoa() */
2    #include <string.h>      /* for memset() */
3
4    #define MAXPENDING 5     /* Maximum outstanding connection requests */
5
6    void DieWithError(char *errorMessage);  /* Error handling function */
7
8    int CreateTCPServerSocket(unsigned short port)
9    {
10       int sock;                           /* socket to create */
11       struct sockaddr_in echoServAddr;    /* Local address */
12
13       /* Create socket for incoming connections */
14       if ((sock = socket(PF_INET, SOCK_STREAM, IPPROTO_TCP)) < 0)
15           DieWithError("socket() failed");
16
17       /* Construct local address structure */
18       memset(&echoServAddr, 0, sizeof(echoServAddr));     /* Zero out structure */
19       echoServAddr.sin_family = AF_INET;                  /* Internet address family */
20       echoServAddr.sin_addr.s_addr = htonl(INADDR_ANY);   /* Any incoming interface */
21       echoServAddr.sin_port = htons(port);                /* Local port */
22
23       /* Bind to the local address */
24       if (bind(sock, (struct sockaddr *) &echoServAddr, sizeof(echoServAddr)) < 0)
25           DieWithError("bind() failed");
26
27       /* Mark the socket so it will listen for incoming connections */
28       if (listen(sock, MAXPENDING) < 0)
29           DieWithError("listen() failed");
30
31       return sock;
32   }
```

CreateTCPServerSocket.c

AcceptTCPConnection.c

```
0   #include <stdio.h>        /* for printf() */
1   #include <sys/socket.h> /* for accept() */
2   #include <arpa/inet.h>  /* for sockaddr_in and inet_ntoa() */
3
4   void DieWithError(char *errorMessage);  /* Error handling function */
5
6   int AcceptTCPConnection(int servSock)
7   {
8       int clntSock;                     /* Socket descriptor for client */
9       struct sockaddr_in echoClntAddr; /* Client address */
10      unsigned int clntLen;             /* Length of client address data structure */
11
12      /* Set the size of the in-out parameter */
13      clntLen = sizeof(echoClntAddr);
14
15      /* Wait for a client to connect */
16      if ((clntSock = accept(servSock, (struct sockaddr *) &echoClntAddr,
17             &clntLen)) < 0)
18          DieWithError("accept() failed");
19
20      /* clntSock is connected to a client! */
21
22      printf("Handling client %s\n", inet_ntoa(echoClntAddr.sin_addr));
23
24      return clntSock;
25  }
```

After connection establishment, references to the child socket are done exclusively through the socket descriptor (*clntSock* in this example). In our forking TCP echo server, the IP address and port of the client are only known temporarily in AcceptTCPConnection(). What if we want to know the IP address and port outside of AcceptTCPConnection()? Of course, we could return that information from AcceptTCPConnection() and retain it in main(); however, sockets provides us with another way to access this information using only the socket descriptor. Given the descriptor for a connected socket, getpeername() returns a **sockaddr** structure containing the remote IP address and port information. A companion function, getsockname(), returns the same type of information for the local IP address and port.

int getpeername(**int** *socket*, **struct sockaddr** *remoteAddress*, **unsigned int** *addressLength*)
int getsockname(**int** *socket*, **struct sockaddr** *localAddress*, **unsigned int** *addressLength*)

socket is the socket descriptor on which to query for address information. *remoteAddress* and *localAddress* are the preallocated **sockaddr_in** structures (cast to **sockaddr** structures) where address information is returned. As with other socket calls using **sockaddr**, the *addressLength* is an in-out parameter specifying the length of the address structure in bytes.

5.4.2 Per-Client Thread

Forking a new process to handle each client works, but it is expensive. Every time a process is created, the operating system must duplicate the entire state of the parent process including memory, stack, file/socket descriptors, and so on. Threads decrease this cost by allowing multitasking within the same process: A newly created thread simply shares the same address space (code and data) with the parent, negating the need to duplicate the parent state.

The next example program, TCPEchoServer-Thread.c, demonstrates a thread-per-client multitasking approach for the TCP echo server using POSIX threads[6] ("PThreads"). The majority of the program is identical to TCPEchoServer-Fork.c (page 61). Again, no changes are required to TCPEchoClient.c (page 13) to work with this new server. The program comments are limited to code that differs from the forking echo server.

TCPEchoServer-Thread.c

```
 0  #include "TCPEchoServer.h"   /* TCP echo server includes */
 1  #include <pthread.h>         /* for POSIX threads */
 2
 3  void *ThreadMain(void *arg);              /* Main program of a thread */
 4
 5  /* Structure of arguments to pass to client thread */
 6  struct ThreadArgs
 7  {
 8      int clntSock;                         /* Socket descriptor for client */
 9  };
10
11  int main(int argc, char *argv[])
12  {
13      int servSock;                    /* Socket descriptor for server */
14      int clntSock;                    /* Socket descriptor for client */
15      unsigned short echoServPort;     /* Server port */
16      pthread_t threadID;              /* Thread ID from pthread_create() */
17      struct ThreadArgs *threadArgs;   /* Pointer to argument structure for thread */
18
```

---

[6] Other thread packages work in generally the same manner. We selected POSIX threads because a port of POSIX threads exists for most operating systems.

```
19      if (argc != 2)     /* Test for correct number of arguments */
20      {
21          fprintf(stderr,"Usage:  %s <SERVER PORT>\n", argv[0]);
22          exit(1);
23      }
24
25      echoServPort = atoi(argv[1]);  /* First arg: local port */
26
27      servSock = CreateTCPServerSocket(echoServPort);
28
29      for (;;) /* run forever */
30      {
31          clntSock = AcceptTCPConnection(servSock);
32
33          /* Create separate memory for client argument */
34          if ((threadArgs = (struct ThreadArgs *) malloc(sizeof(struct ThreadArgs)))
35                  == NULL)
36              DieWithError("malloc() failed");
37          threadArgs -> clntSock = clntSock;
38
39          /* Create client thread */
40          if (pthread_create(&threadID, NULL, ThreadMain, (void *) threadArgs) != 0)
41              DieWithError("pthread_create() failed");
42          printf("with thread %ld\n", (long int) threadID);
43      }
44      /* NOT REACHED */
45  }
46
47  void *ThreadMain(void *threadArgs)
48  {
49      int clntSock;                    /* Socket descriptor for client connection */
50
51      /* Guarantees that thread resources are deallocated upon return */
52      pthread_detach(pthread_self());
53
54      /* Extract socket file descriptor from argument */
55      clntSock = ((struct ThreadArgs *) threadArgs) -> clntSock;
56      free(threadArgs);                /* Deallocate memory for argument */
57
58      HandleTCPClient(clntSock);
59
60      return (NULL);
61  }
```

TCPEchoServer-Thread.c

1. **Additional include file for POSIX thread:** line 1

2. **Set up for threads:** lines 3-9
   TheadMain() is the function for the POSIX thread to execute. pthread_create() allows the caller to pass *one* pointer as an argument to the function executed by the new thread. The ThreadArgs structure contains the "real" list of parameters. The process creating a new thread allocates and populates the structure before calling pthread_create(). In this program the thread function only needs a single argument (clntSock), so we could have simply passed a pointer to an integer; however, the ThreadArgs structure provides a more general framework for thread argument passing.

3. **Population of thread argument structure:** lines 34-37
   We only pass the client socket descriptor to the new thread.

4. **Invocation of the new thread:** lines 40-42

5. **Thread execution:** lines 47-61
   ThreadMain is the function called by pthread_create() when it creates a new thread. The required prototype for the function to be executed by a thread is **void** *fcn*(**void** *), a function that takes a single argument of type **void** * and returns a **void** *.

   - **Thread detach:** line 52
     By default when a thread's main function returns, state is maintained about the function return code until the parent harvests the results. This is very similar to the behavior for processes. pthread_detach() allows the thread state to be immediately deallocated upon completion without parent intervention. pthread_self() provides the thread ID of the current thread as a parameter to pthread_detach(), much in the way that getpid() provides a process its process ID.

   - **Extracting the parameters from the ThreadArgs structure:** lines 55-56
     The ThreadArgs structure for this program only contains the socket descriptor of the socket connected to the client socket by accept(). Because the ThreadArgs structure is allocated on a per-connection basis, the new thread can deallocate threadArgs once the parameter(s) have been extracted.

   - **HandleTCPClient:** line 58
     The thread function calls the same HandleTCPClient() function that we have been using all along.

   - **Thread return:** line 60
     After creation, the parent does not need to communicate with the thread, so the thread can return a NULL pointer.

Because the parent and thread share the same address space (and thus file/socket descriptors), the parent thread and the per-connection thread do not close the connection and listening sockets, respectively, before proceeding, as the parent and child processes did in the forking example. Figure 5.2 illustrates the actions of the threaded TCP echo server. There are a few disadvantages to using threads instead of processes:

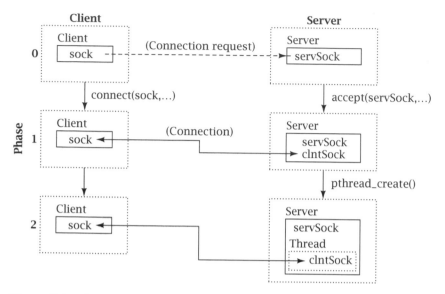

Figure 5.2: Threaded TCP echo server.

- If a child process goes awry, it is easy to monitor and kill it from the command line using its process identifier. Threads do not always provide this capability, so additional server functionality must be provided to monitor and kill individual threads.

- If the operating system is oblivious to the notion of threads, it may schedule by giving an equivalent time slice to every process. In this case, a threaded Web server with 1000 threads may get the same amount of CPU time as the game Minesweeper.

5.4.3 Constrained Multitasking

Process and thread creation both incur overhead. In addition, the scheduling and context switching among many processes or threads creates extra work for a system. As the number of processes or threads increases, the operating system spends more and more time dealing with this overhead. Eventually, the point is reached where adding an additional process or thread actually decreases overall performance. That is, a client might experience shorter service time if its connection request were queued until some preceding client finished, instead of creating a new process or thread to service it.

We can avoid this problem by limiting the number of processes created by the server, which we call *constrained-multitasking servers*. (We present a solution for processes, but it is directly applicable to threads.) In this solution, the server begins as the other servers by creating, binding, and listening to a socket. Then the server creates a set number (say, N) of processes, each of which loops forever, accepting connections from the (same) listening socket. This works because when multiple processes call accept() on the same listening socket at the same time, they all block until a connection is established. Then the system picks one process, and the socket descriptor for that new connection is returned *only in that process*; the others remain blocked until the next connection is established, another lucky winner is chosen, and so on.

Our next example program, TCPEchoServer-ForkN.c, implements this server model as a modification of the original TCPEchoServer.c (page 19), so we only comment on the differences.

TCPEchoServer-ForkN.c

```
0   #include "TCPEchoServer.h"
1
2   void ProcessMain(int servSock);          /* Main program of process */
3
4   int main(int argc, char *argv[])
5   {
6       int servSock;                        /* Socket descriptor for server*/
7       unsigned short echoServPort;         /* Server port */
8       pid_t processID;                     /* Process ID */
9       unsigned int processLimit;           /* Number of child processes to create */
10      unsigned int processCt;              /* Process counter */
11
12      if (argc != 3)      /* Test for correct number of arguments */
13      {
14          fprintf(stderr,"Usage:  %s <SERVER PORT> <FORK LIMIT>\n", argv[0]);
15          exit(1);
16      }
17
18      echoServPort = atoi(argv[1]),  /* First arg: local port */
19      processLimit = atoi(argv[2]);  /* Second arg: number of child processes */
20
21      servSock = CreateTCPServerSocket(echoServPort);
22
23      for (processCt=0; processCt < processLimit; processCt++)
24          /* Fork child process and report any errors */
25          if ((processID = fork()) < 0)
26              DieWithError("fork() failed");
27          else if (processID == 0)  /* If this is the child process */
28              ProcessMain(servSock);
29
30      exit(0);  /* The children will carry on */
31  }
32
33  void ProcessMain(int servSock)
34  {
35      int clntSock;                        /* Socket descriptor for client connection */
```

```
36
37      for (;;)  /* Loop forever */
38      {
39          clntSock = AcceptTCPConnection(servSock);
40          printf("with child process: %d\n", (unsigned int) getpid());
41          HandleTCPClient(clntSock);
42      }
43  }
```

TCPEchoServer-ForkN.c

1. **Prototype for "main" of forked process:** line 2
   Each of the N processes executes the ProcessMain() function.

2. **Spawning *processLimit* processes:** lines 23–28
   Execute loop *processLimit* times, each time forking a process that calls ProcessMain() with *servSock* as the parameter.

3. **Parent exits after spawning children:** line 30

4. **ProcessMain():** lines 33–43
   ProcessMain() runs forever handling client requests. Effectively, it is the same as the for(;;) loop in TCPEchoServer.c (page 19).

Because only N processes are created, we save in scheduling overhead, and because each process lives forever handling client requests, we save in process creation overhead. Of course, if we spawn too few processes, we can still have clients waiting unnecessarily for service.

5.5 Multiplexing

Our programs so far have dealt with I/O over a single channel; each version of our echo server deals with only one client connection at a time. However, it is often the case that an application needs the ability to do I/O on multiple channels simultaneously. For example, we might want to provide echo service on several ports at once. The problem with this becomes clear as soon as you consider what happens after the server creates and binds a socket to each port. It is ready to accept() connections, but which socket to choose? A call to accept() (or recv()) on one socket may block, causing established connections to another socket to wait unnecessarily. This problem can be solved using nonblocking sockets, but in that case the server ends up continuously polling the sockets, which is wasteful. We would like to let the server block until *some* socket is ready for I/O.

Fortunately, UNIX provides a way to do this. With the select function, a program can specify a list of descriptors to check for pending I/O; select() suspends the program until one of the descriptors in the list becomes ready to perform I/O and returns an indication of which descriptors are ready. Then the program can proceed with I/O on that descriptor with the assurance that the operation will not block.

---

int select(**int** *maxDescPlus1*, **fd_set** **readDescs*, **fd_set** **writeDescs*, **fd_set** **exceptionDescs*,
    struct timeval **timeout*)

---

select() monitors three separate lists of descriptors that, typically, are implemented as vectors of bits:

readDescs: Descriptors in this vector are checked for immediate input data availability.

writeDescs: Descriptors in this vector are checked for the ability to immediately write data.

exceptionDescs: Descriptors in this vector are checked for pending exceptions.

Passing NULL for any of the descriptor vectors makes select() ignore that type of I/O. For example, passing NULL for *exceptionDescs* causes select() to completely ignore exceptions on any sockets. The **fd_set** descriptor lists are manipulated by four system-provided macros:

FD_ZERO(**fd_set** **descriptorVector*)
FD_CLR(**int** *descriptor*, **fd_set** **descriptorVector*)
FD_SET(**int** *descriptor*, **fd_set** **descriptorVector*)
FD_ISSET(**int** *descriptor*, **fd_set** **descriptorVector*)

FD_ZERO removes all descriptors from the vector. FD_CLR() and FD_SET() remove and add descriptors to the vector. Vector membership of a descriptor is tested by FD_ISSET().

Though the maximum number of descriptors can be quite large, most applications use very few descriptors. To avoid making select() search all possible vector positions for all three vectors, we give it a hint by specifying in *maxDescPlus1* the maximum number of descriptor values to consider in each descriptor vector. Since descriptors begin at 0, the number of descriptors is always the maximum descriptor value plus one. For example, if descriptors 0, 3, and 5 are set in the descriptor list, the number of descriptors for select() to consider is 6 (0 through 5), which is also the maximum descriptor value (5) plus one. Notice that we set *maxDescPlus1* for *all* three descriptor lists. If the exception descriptor list has the largest descriptor value, say, 7, then we set *maxDescPlus1* to 8, irrespective of the descriptor values set for read and write.

What would you pay for the ability to listen to so many descriptors for up to *three* types of I/O? Don't answer yet because select() does even more! The last parameter (*timeout*) allows

control over how long select() will wait for something to happen. The *timeout* is specified
with a **timeval** data structure:

```
struct timeval
{
    time_t tv_sec;      /* Seconds */
    time_t tv_usec;     /* Microseconds */
};
```

If the time specified in the timeval structure elapses before any of the specified descriptors becomes ready for I/O, select() returns the value 0. If *timeout* is NULL, select() has
no timeout bound and waits until some descriptor becomes ready. Setting both *tv_sec* and
tv_usec to 0 causes select() to return immediately, enabling polling of I/O descriptors.

If no errors occur, select() returns the total number of descriptors prepared for I/O.
To indicate the descriptors ready for I/O, select() changes the descriptor lists so that only
the positions corresponding to ready descriptors are set. For example, if descriptors 0, 3, and
5 are set in the read descriptor list, the write and exception descriptor lists are NULL, and
descriptors 0 and 5 have data available for reading, select() returns 2, and only positions 0
and 5 are set in the returned read descriptor list. An error in select() is indicated by a return
value of −1.

Let's reconsider the problem of running the echo service on multiple ports. If we create
a socket for each port, we could list these sockets in a *readDescriptor* list. A call to select(),
given such a list, would suspend the program until an echo request arrives for at least one
of the descriptors. We could then handle the connection setup and echo for that particular
socket. Our next example program, TCPEchoServer-Select.c, implements this model. The user
can specify an arbitrary number of ports to monitor. Notice that a connection request is
considered I/O and prepares a socket descriptor for reading by select(). To illustrate that
select() works on nonsocket descriptors as well, this server also watches for input from the
standard input stream, which it interprets as a signal to terminate itself.

TCPEchoServer-Select.c

```
 0  #include "TCPEchoServer.h"  /* TCP echo server includes */
 1  #include <sys/time.h>        /* for struct timeval {} */
 2  #include <fcntl.h>           /* for fcntl() */
 3
 4  int main(int argc, char *argv[])
 5  {
 6      int *servSock;                 /* Socket descriptors for server */
 7      int maxDescriptor;             /* Maximum socket descriptor value */
 8      fd_set sockSet;                /* Set of socket descriptors for select() */
 9      long timeout;                  /* Timeout value given on command line */
10      struct timeval selTimeout;     /* Timeout for select() */
11      int running = 1;               /* 1 if server should be running; 0 otherwise */
12      int noPorts;                   /* Number of ports specified on command line */
```

```
13      int port;                          /* Looping variable for ports */
14      unsigned short portNo;             /* Actual port number */
15
16      if (argc < 3)      /* Test for correct number of arguments */
17      {
18          fprintf(stderr, "Usage:  %s <Timeout (secs.)> <Port 1> ...\n", argv[0]);
19          exit(1);
20      }
21
22      timeout = atol(argv[1]);           /* First arg: timeout (secs) */
23      noPorts = argc - 2;                /* Number of ports is argument count minus 2 */
24
25      /* Allocate list of sockets for incoming connections */
26      servSock = (int *) malloc(noPorts * sizeof(int));
27      /* Initialize maxDescriptor for use by select() */
28      maxDescriptor = -1;
29
30      /* Create list of ports and sockets to handle ports */
31      for (port = 0; port < noPorts; port++)
32      {
33          /* Add port to port list */
34          portNo = atoi(argv[port + 2]);  /* Skip first two arguments */
35
36          /* Create port socket */
37          servSock[port] = CreateTCPServerSocket(portNo);
38
39          /* Determine if new descriptor is the largest */
40          if (servSock[port] > maxDescriptor)
41              maxDescriptor = servSock[port];
42      }
43
44      printf("Starting server:  Hit return to shutdown\n");
45      while (running)
46      {
47          /* Zero socket descriptor vector and set for server sockets */
48          /* This must be reset every time select() is called */
49          FD_ZERO(&sockSet);
50          /* Add keyboard to descriptor vector */
51          FD_SET(STDIN_FILENO, &sockSet);
52          for (port = 0; port < noPorts; port++)
53              FD_SET(servSock[port], &sockSet);
54
55          /* Timeout specification */
56          /* This must be reset every time select() is called */
57          selTimeout.tv_sec = timeout;       /* timeout (secs.) */
58          selTimeout.tv_usec = 0;            /* 0 microseconds */
59
```

```
60          /* Suspend program until descriptor is ready or timeout */
61          if (select(maxDescriptor + 1, &sockSet, NULL, NULL, &selTimeout) == 0)
62              printf("No echo requests for %ld secs...Server still alive\n", timeout);
63          else
64          {
65              if (FD_ISSET(STDIN_FILENO, &sockSet)) /* Check keyboard */
66              {
67                  printf("Shutting down server\n");
68                  getchar();
69                  running = 0;
70              }
71
72              for (port = 0; port < noPorts; port++)
73                  if (FD_ISSET(servSock[port], &sockSet))
74                  {
75                      printf("Request on port %d:  ", port);
76                      HandleTCPClient(AcceptTCPConnection(servSock[port]));
77                  }
78          }
79      }
80
81      /* Close sockets */
82      for (port = 0; port < noPorts; port++)
83          close(servSock[port]);
84
85      /* Free list of sockets */
86      free(servSock);
87
88      exit(0);
89  }
```

TCPEchoServer-Select.c

1. **Set up a socket for each port:** lines 31-42

2. **Create list of file descriptors for select():** lines 49-53

3. **Set timer for select():** lines 57-58

4. **select() execution:** lines 61-78

   - **Handle timeout:** line 62
   - **Check keyboard descriptor:** lines 65-70
     If the user presses return, descriptor STDIN_FILENO will be ready for reading; in that case the server terminates itself.

■ **Check the socket descriptors:** lines 72–77
  Test each descriptor, accepting and handling the valid connections.

5. **Wrap up:** lines 82–86
  Close all ports and free memory.

`select()` is a powerful function. It can also be used to implement a timeout version of any of the blocking I/O functions (e.g., `recv()`, `accept()`) without using alarms.

5.6 Multiple Recipients

So far, all of our sockets have dealt with communication between two entities, usually a server and a client. Such one-to-one communication is called *unicast* because only one ("uni") copy of the data is sent ("cast"). In some cases, information is of interest to multiple recipients. We could simply unicast a copy of the data to each recipient; however, this may be very inefficient. Consider the case where the sender connects to the Internet over a single path. Unicasting multiple copies over that single connection creates duplication, wasting bandwidth. In fact, if each unicast connection across this shared path requires a fixed amount of bandwidth, there is a hard limit to the number of receivers we can support. For example, if a video server sends 1-Mbps streams and the server's network connection is only 3 Mbps (a healthy connection rate), it can only support three simultaneous users.

Fortunately, the network provides a way to more efficiently use bandwidth. Instead of making the sender responsible for duplicating packets, we can give this job to the network. In our video server example, we send only a single copy of the stream across the server's connection to the network, which duplicates the data only when appropriate. With this model of duplication, the server uses only 1 Mbps across its connection to the network, irrespective of the number of clients.

There are two types of network duplication: *broadcast* and *multicast*. With broadcast, all hosts on the network receive a copy of the message. A broadcast message is indiscriminately sent to everyone on the network. A multicast message is sent to some (potentially empty) subset of all the hosts on the network. Obviously, broadcast is just a special case of multicast, where the subset of receivers contains all of the hosts on the network. For IP, *only UDP sockets* are allowed to broadcast and multicast.

5.6.1 Broadcast

Broadcasting UDP datagrams is similar to sending unicast datagrams. The main distinction between the use of broadcast and unicast is the form of the address. In practice, there are two types of broadcast address: *local broadcast* and *directed broadcast*. A local broadcast address (255.255.255.255) sends the message to every host on the same broadcast network. Local broadcast messages are never forwarded by routers. A host on an Ethernet LAN can send a message to all other hosts on that same LAN, but the message will not be forwarded by a router so no other hosts may receive it. Directed broadcast allows broadcast to all hosts on a specific network. IP addresses have two parts: the network and the host identifier. If the network identifier is X, a directed broadcast address for that network is an IP address with the high-order bits set to X and the remaining bits set to 1 (i.e., X111 . . . 111). For example, the directed broadcast address for a network with network identifier 169.125 (first two bytes) is 169.125.255.255. With subnetting, we consider the subnet identifier part of the network identifier, so the definition of a directed broadcast address for a subnet is the same. For example, if a network with subnet mask 255.255.255.0 has a subnet 169.125.134, the directed broadcast address for that subnet is 169.125.134.255.

What about a network-wide broadcast address to send a message to all hosts? There is no such address. To see why, consider the impact on the network of a broadcast to every host on the Internet. The send of a single datagram would result in a very, very large number of packet duplications by the routers, and bandwidth would be consumed on each and every network. The consequences of misuse (malicious or accidental) are too great, so the designers of IP left out such an Internet-wide broadcast facility on purpose. Even with these restrictions, network-scoped broadcast can be very useful. Often, it is used in state exchange for network games where the players are all on the same broadcast LAN network.

We create a sender and receiver to demonstrate the use of UDP broadcast, as shown in BroadcastSender.c. Our sender broadcasts a given string every three seconds to the specified broadcast address.

BroadcastSender.c

```
0   #include <stdio.h>        /* for printf() and fprintf() */
1   #include <sys/socket.h>  /* for socket() and bind() */
2   #include <arpa/inet.h>   /* for sockaddr_in */
3   #include <stdlib.h>       /* for atoi() */
4   #include <string.h>       /* for memset() */
5   #include <unistd.h>       /* for close() */
6
7   void DieWithError(char *errorMessage);  /* External error handling function */
8
9   int main(int argc, char *argv[])
10  {
11      int sock;                         /* Socket */
12      struct sockaddr_in broadcastAddr; /* Broadcast address */
13      char *broadcastIP;                /* IP broadcast address */
14      unsigned short broadcastPort;     /* Server port */
15      char *sendString;                 /* String to broadcast */
16      int broadcastPermission;          /* Socket opt to set permission to broadcast */
17      unsigned int sendStringLen;       /* Length of string to broadcast */
18
19      if (argc < 4)                     /* Test for correct number of parameters */
20      {
21          fprintf(stderr,"Usage:  %s <IP Address> <Port> <Send String>\n", argv[0]);
```

```
22          exit(1);
23      }
24
25      broadcastIP = argv[1];              /* First arg: broadcast IP address */
26      broadcastPort = atoi(argv[2]);      /* Second arg: broadcast port */
27      sendString = argv[3];               /* Third arg: string to broadcast */
28
29      /* Create socket for sending/receiving datagrams */
30      if ((sock = socket(AF_INET, SOCK_DGRAM, IPPROTO_UDP)) < 0)
31          DieWithError("socket() failed");
32
33      /* Set socket to allow broadcast */
34      broadcastPermission = 1;
35      if (setsockopt(sock, SOL_SOCKET, SO_BROADCAST, (void *) &broadcastPermission,
36              sizeof(broadcastPermission)) < 0)
37          DieWithError("setsockopt() failed");
38
39      /* Construct local address structure */
40      memset(&broadcastAddr, 0, sizeof(broadcastAddr));   /* Zero out structure */
41      broadcastAddr.sin_family = AF_INET;                 /* Internet address family */
42      broadcastAddr.sin_addr.s_addr = inet_addr(broadcastIP);/* Broadcast IP address */
43      broadcastAddr.sin_port = htons(broadcastPort);      /* Broadcast port */
44
45      sendStringLen = strlen(sendString);  /* Find length of sendString */
46      for (;;) /* Run forever */
47      {
48          /* Broadcast sendString in datagram to clients every 3 seconds*/
49          if (sendto(sock, sendString, sendStringLen, 0, (struct sockaddr *)
50                  &broadcastAddr, sizeof(broadcastAddr)) != sendStringLen)
51              DieWithError("sendto() sent a different number of bytes than expected");
52
53          sleep(3);   /* Avoids flooding the network */
54      }
55      /* NOT REACHED */
56  }
```

BroadcastSender.c

1. **Setting permission to broadcast:** lines 34–37
   By default, sockets cannot broadcast. Setting SO_BROADCAST for the socket enables socket broadcast.

2. **Repeatedly broadcast:** lines 46–54

Our receiver waits to receive a single broadcast message, prints the message, and exits.

BroadcastReceiver.c

```
0   #include <stdio.h>        /* for printf() and fprintf() */
1   #include <sys/socket.h>   /* for socket(), connect(), sendto(), and recvfrom() */
2   #include <arpa/inet.h>    /* for sockaddr_in and inet_addr() */
3   #include <stdlib.h>       /* for atoi() */
4   #include <string.h>       /* for memset() */
5   #include <unistd.h>       /* for close() */
6
7   #define MAXRECVSTRING 255  /* Longest string to receive */
8
9   void DieWithError(char *errorMessage);  /* External error handling function */
10
11  int main(int argc, char *argv[])
12  {
13      int sock;                        /* Socket */
14      struct sockaddr_in broadcastAddr; /* Broadcast Address */
15      unsigned int broadcastPort;      /* Port */
16      char recvString[MAXRECVSTRING+1]; /* Buffer for received string */
17      int recvStringLen;               /* Length of received string */
18
19      if (argc != 2)     /* Test for correct number of arguments */
20      {
21          fprintf(stderr,"Usage: %s <Broadcast Port>\n", argv[0]);
22          exit(1);
23      }
24
25      broadcastPort = atoi(argv[1]);    /* First arg: broadcast port */
26
27      /* Create a best-effort datagram socket using UDP */
28      if ((sock = socket(AF_INET, SOCK_DGRAM, IPPROTO_UDP)) < 0)
29          DieWithError("socket() failed");
30
31      /* Construct bind structure */
32      memset(&broadcastAddr, 0, sizeof(broadcastAddr));   /* Zero out structure */
33      broadcastAddr.sin_family = AF_INET;                 /* Internet address family */
34      broadcastAddr.sin_addr.s_addr = htonl(INADDR_ANY);  /* Any incoming interface */
35      broadcastAddr.sin_port = htons(broadcastPort);      /* Broadcast port */
36
37      /* Bind to the broadcast port */
38      if (bind(sock, (struct sockaddr *) &broadcastAddr, sizeof(broadcastAddr)) < 0)
39          DieWithError("bind() failed");
40
41      /* Receive a single datagram from the server */
42      if ((recvStringLen = recvfrom(sock, recvString, MAXRECVSTRING, 0, NULL, 0)) < 0)
```

```
43              DieWithError("recvfrom() failed");
44
45          recvString[recvStringLen] = '\0';
46          printf("Received: %s\n", recvString);     /* Print the received string */
47
48          close(sock);
49          exit(0);
50      }
```

BroadcastReceiver.c

5.6.2 Multicast

As with broadcast, UDP multicast is very similar to UDP unicast. Again, the main difference is the form of the address. A multicast address identifies a set of receivers for multicast messages. The designers of IP allocated a range of the address space dedicated to multicast. These are class D addresses and range from 224.0.0.0 to 239.255.255.255. With the exception of a few reserved multicast addresses, a sender can send datagrams addressed to any class D address.

Our next example, MulticastSender.c, implements the multicast version of the broadcast sender by multicasting a UDP datagram to a specific multicast address every three seconds:

MulticastSender.c

```
0   #include <stdio.h>       /* for fprintf() */
1   #include <sys/socket.h>  /* for socket(), connect(), send(), and recv() */
2   #include <arpa/inet.h>   /* for sockaddr_in and inet_addr() */
3   #include <stdlib.h>       /* for atoi() */
4   #include <string.h>       /* for memset() */
5   #include <unistd.h>       /* for sleep() */
6
7   void DieWithError(char *errorMessage);  /* External error handling function */
8
9   int main(int argc, char *argv[])
10  {
11      int sock;                    /* Socket */
12      struct sockaddr_in multicastAddr; /* Multicast address */
13      char *multicastIP;           /* IP Multicast address */
14      unsigned short multicastPort;   /* Server port */
15      char *sendString;            /* String to multicast */
16      unsigned char multicastTTL;  /* TTL of multicast packets */
17      unsigned int sendStringLen;  /* Length of string to multicast */
18
```

```
19      if ((argc < 4) || (argc > 5))           /* Test for correct number of parameters */
20      {
21          fprintf(stderr,"Usage:  %s <IP Address> <Port> <Send String> [<TTL>]\n",
22                  argv[0]);
23          exit(1);
24      }
25
26      multicastIP = argv[1];              /* First arg: multicast IP address */
27      multicastPort = atoi(argv[2]);     /* Second arg: multicast port */
28      sendString = argv[3];              /* Third arg: string to multicast */
29
30      if (argc == 5)                     /* Is TTL specified on command line? */
31          multicastTTL = atoi(argv[4]);  /* Command line specified TTL */
32      else
33          multicastTTL = 1;              /* Default TTL = 1 */
34
35      /* Create socket for sending/receiving datagrams */
36      if ((sock = socket(AF_INET, SOCK_DGRAM, IPPROTO_UDP)) < 0)
37          DieWithError("socket() failed");
38
39      /* Set TTL of multicast packet */
40      if (setsockopt(sock, IPPROTO_IP, IP_MULTICAST_TTL, (void *) &multicastTTL,
41              sizeof(multicastTTL)) < 0)
42          DieWithError("setsockopt() failed");
43
44      /* Construct local address structure */
45      memset(&multicastAddr, 0, sizeof(multicastAddr));   /* Zero out structure */
46      multicastAddr.sin_family = AF_INET;                 /* Internet address family */
47      multicastAddr.sin_addr.s_addr = inet_addr(multicastIP);/* Multicast IP address */
48      multicastAddr.sin_port = htons(multicastPort);      /* Multicast port */
49
50      sendStringLen = strlen(sendString);  /* Find length of sendString */
51      for (;;) /* run forever */
52      {
53          /* Multicast sendString in datagram to clients every 3 seconds*/
54          if (sendto(sock, sendString, sendStringLen, 0, (struct sockaddr *)
55              &multicastAddr, sizeof(multicastAddr)) != sendStringLen)
56            DieWithError("sendto() sent a different number of bytes than expected");
57          sleep(3);
58      }
59      /* NOT REACHED */
60  }
```

MulticastSender.c

The only significant differences between our broadcast and multicast senders are (1) the multicast sender does not need to set the permission to multicast and (2) we set the TTL (time-to-live) for multicast. Every IP packet contains a TTL, initialized to some default value and decremented by each router that handles the packet. When the TTL reaches 0, the packet is discarded. By setting the TTL, we limit the number of hops a multicast packet can traverse from the sender. We can change the default TTL value by setting a socket option. The TTL may also be set for broadcast; however, since routers generally do not forward broadcast packets, it usually has no effect.

Unlike broadcast, network multicast duplicates the message only to a specific set of receivers. This set of receivers, called a *multicast group*, is identified by a shared multicast (or group) address. These receivers need some mechanism to notify the network of their interest in receiving data sent to a particular multicast address. Once notified, the network can begin forwarding the multicast messages to the receiver. This notification, called "joining a group," is accomplished with a multicast request sent by the sockets interface. Our multicast receiver joins a specified group, receives and prints a single multicast message from that group, and exits.

MulticastReceiver.c

```
0   #include <stdio.h>       /* for printf() and fprintf() */
1   #include <sys/socket.h> /* for socket(), connect(), sendto(), and recvfrom() */
2   #include <arpa/inet.h>   /* for sockaddr_in and inet_addr() */
3   #include <stdlib.h>      /* for atoi() */
4   #include <string.h>      /* for memset() */
5   #include <unistd.h>      /* for close() */
6
7   #define MAXRECVSTRING 255  /* Longest string to receive */
8
9   void DieWithError(char *errorMessage);  /* External error handling function */
10
11  int main(int argc, char *argv[])
12  {
13      int sock;                       /* Socket */
14      struct sockaddr_in multicastAddr; /* Multicast Address */
15      char *multicastIP;              /* IP Multicast Address */
16      unsigned int multicastPort;     /* Port */
17      char recvString[MAXRECVSTRING+1]; /* Buffer for received string */
18      unsigned int recvStringLen;     /* Length of received string */
19      struct ip_mreq multicastRequest; /* Multicast address join structure */
20
21      if (argc != 3)     /* Test for correct number of arguments */
22      {
23          fprintf(stderr,"Usage: %s <Multicast IP> <Multicast Port>\n", argv[0]);
```

```
24          exit(1);
25      }
26
27      multicastIP = argv[1];          /* First arg: multicast IP address (dotted quad) */
28      multicastPort = atoi(argv[2]);/* Second arg: multicast port */
29
30      /* Create a best-effort datagram socket using UDP */
31      if ((sock = socket(AF_INET, SOCK_DGRAM, IPPROTO_UDP)) < 0)
32          DieWithError("socket() failed");
33
34      /* Construct bind structure */
35      memset(&multicastAddr, 0, sizeof(multicastAddr));   /* Zero out structure */
36      multicastAddr.sin_family = AF_INET;                 /* Internet address family */
37      multicastAddr.sin_addr.s_addr = htonl(INADDR_ANY);  /* Any incoming interface */
38      multicastAddr.sin_port = htons(multicastPort);      /* Multicast port */
39
40      /* Bind to the multicast port */
41      if (bind(sock, (struct sockaddr *) &multicastAddr, sizeof(multicastAddr)) < 0)
42          DieWithError("bind() failed");
43
44      /* Specify the multicast group */
45      multicastRequest.imr_multiaddr.s_addr = inet_addr(multicastIP);
46      /* Accept multicast from any interface */
47      multicastRequest.imr_interface.s_addr = htonl(INADDR_ANY);
48      /* Join the multicast group */
49      if (setsockopt(sock, IPPROTO_IP, IP_ADD_MEMBERSHIP, (void *) &multicastRequest,
50              sizeof(multicastRequest)) < 0)
51          DieWithError("setsockopt() failed");
52
53      /* Receive a single datagram from the server */
54      if ((recvStringLen = recvfrom(sock, recvString, MAXRECVSTRING, 0, NULL, 0)) < 0)
55          DieWithError("recvfrom() failed");
56
57      recvString[recvStringLen] = '\0';
58      printf("Received: %s\n", recvString);    /* Print the received string */
59
60      close(sock);
61      exit(0);
62  }
```

MulticastReceiver.c

The only significant difference between our multicast and broadcast receiver is that the multicast receiver must join the multicast group. The multicast receiver specifies the group address with the **ip_mreq** structure.

```
struct ip_mreq
{
    struct in_addr imr_multiaddr;  /* Group multicast address */
    struct in_addr imr_interface;  /* Local interface address */
};
```

imr_multiaddr contains the network-byte-ordered Internet address for the group (e.g., 224.1.2.3). imr_interface specifies the host interface to join the group. INADDR_ANY allows the join from any interface. Once specified, the **ip_mreq** structure is given as the parameter for the IP_ADD_MEMBERSHIP option.

5.6.3 Broadcast vs. Multicast

The decision of using broadcast or multicast in an application depends on several issues, including the portion of network hosts interested in receiving the data and the knowledge of the communicating parties. Broadcast works well if a large percentage of the network hosts wish to receive the message; however, if there are many more hosts than receivers, broadcast is very inefficient. In the Internet, broadcasting would be very expensive even if the communication had 10,000 interested receivers because the data would have to be duplicated to every host on the Internet (well over 10,000). In this case, multicast limits the duplication of data for delivery to only the networks that have hosts interested in the message. Because of the negative consequences of Internet-wide broadcast, most routers do not forward broadcast packets; thus, applications are generally limited to LAN broadcasts only.

The disadvantage of multicast is that IP multicast receivers must know the address of a multicast group to join. Knowledge of an address is not required for broadcast. In some contexts, this makes broadcast a better mechanism for discovery than multicast. All hosts can receive broadcast by default, so it is simple to ask all hosts a question like "Where's the printer?"

Thought Questions

1. State precisely the conditions under which an iterative server is preferable to a multi-processing server.

2. Would you ever need to implement a timeout in a client or server that uses TCP?

3. How can you determine the minimum and maximum allowable sizes for a socket's send and receive buffers? Determine the minimums for your system.

4. Why do you think the default behavior for SIGPIPE is to terminate the program? (Consider what might happen if it were ignored.)

Under the Hood

Some of the subtleties of the sockets programming interface are difficult to grasp without some understanding of the data structures associated with each socket in the implementation and some details of how the underlying protocols work. This is especially true of TCP sockets. This chapter describes some of what goes on "under the hood" when you create and use a socket. Please note that this description covers only the normal sequence of events and glosses over many details. Nevertheless, we believe that even this basic level of understanding is helpful. Readers who want the full story are referred to the TCP specification [12] or to one of the more comprehensive treatises on the subject [3, 20].

Figure 6.1 is a simplified view of the data structures associated with a socket. The program refers to these structures via the *descriptor* returned by socket(). This is best thought of as simply a "handle" that is linked to an underlying socket structure. As the figure indicates, more than one descriptor can refer to the same socket structure. In fact, descriptors in *different processes* can refer to the same underlying socket structure. By "socket structure" here we mean all data structures in the socket layer and TCP implementation that contain state information relevant to this socket abstraction. Thus, the socket structure contains send and receive queues and other information, including the following:

- The *local and remote* Internet addresses and port numbers associated with the socket. The local Internet address (labeled "Local IP" in the figure) is one of those assigned to the local host; the local port is either set with bind() or chosen arbitrarily by the implementation when the socket is first used. The remote address and port identify the remote socket, if any, to which the socket is connected. We will see more about how they are set in Section 6.4.

- A FIFO queue of received data waiting to be delivered to the program, and possibly a queue of data waiting for transmission.

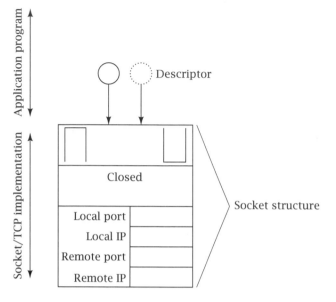

Figure 6.1: Data structures associated with a TCP socket.

■ For a TCP socket, additional *protocol state* information relevant to the opening and closing TCP handshakes. In Figure 6.1, the state is "Closed"; all sockets start out in the Closed state.

Knowing about the existence of these data structures and how they are affected by the underlying protocols is useful because they control various aspects of the behavior of the sockets API functions. For example, because TCP provides a *reliable* byte-stream service, a copy of any data passed in a send() must be kept until it has been successfully received at the other end. When the send() returns, the program cannot know whether the data has actually been sent or not—only that it has been copied into the local buffer. Moreover, the nature of the byte-stream service means that message boundaries are *not* preserved in the receive queue. As we saw earlier (Section 3.4), this complicates the process of receiving and parsing for some protocols. On the other hand, with a UDP socket, packets are *not* buffered for retransmission, and by the time a call to sendto() returns, the message has been given to the network subsystem for transmission. If the network subsystem cannot handle the message for some reason, the message is silently dropped (this is rare). However, as we discussed in Chapter 4, message boundaries *are* preserved in UDP's receive queue; a single call to recvfrom() will *never* return data from more than one received message.

Sections 6.1, 6.2, and 6.3 deal with some of the subtleties of sending and receiving with TCP's byte-stream service. Then in Section 6.4 we consider the connection establishment and termination of the TCP protocol. Finally, in Section 6.5 we discuss the process of matching incoming packets to sockets and the rules about bind()ing to port numbers.

6.1 Buffering and TCP

As a programmer, the most important thing to remember when using a TCP socket is this:

You cannot assume any correspondence between send()s and recv()s.

In particular, data passed in a single send() can be returned by multiple recv()s at the other end, and a single call to recv() may return data passed in multiple send()s. To see this, consider a program that does the following:

```
rv = connect(s,...);
.
.
.
rv = send(s,buffer0,1000,0);
.
.
.
rv = send(s,buffer1,2000,0);
.
.
.
rv = send(s,buffer2,5000,0);
.
.
.
close(s);
```

where the ellipses represent code that sets up the buffers but contains no other calls to send(). This TCP connection transfers 8000 bytes to the receiver. The way these 8000 bytes are grouped for delivery at the receiving end of the connection depends on the timing between the calls to send() and recv() at the two ends of the connection (as well as the size of the buffers provided to the recv() calls).

We can think of the sequence of all bytes sent (in one direction) on a TCP connection up to a particular instant in time as being divided into three FIFO "queues":

1. **SendQ**: Bytes buffered in the sockets layer at the sender that have not yet been successfully transmitted to the receiving host.

2. **RecvQ**: Bytes buffered in the sockets layer at the receiver waiting to be delivered to the receiving program, that is, waiting to be returned via recv().

3. **Delivered**: Bytes already returned to the receiving program via recv().

A call to send() appends bytes to **SendQ**.[1] The TCP protocol is responsible for moving bytes—in order—from **SendQ** to **RecvQ**. It is important to realize that this transfer cannot be

---

[1] The default behavior for stream sockets is for a call send(s, buffer, n, 0) to block until all n bytes have been transferred to **SendQ**. This behavior can be changed by making the socket nonblocking or by using a nonblocking send() call (see Section 5.3). However, in that case the call may return −1 and errno is set to EWOULDBLOCK.

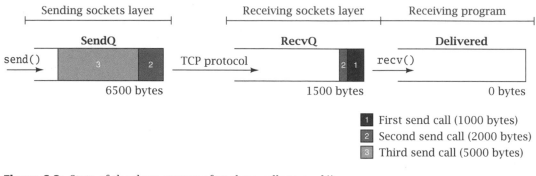

Figure 6.2: State of the three queues after three calls to send().

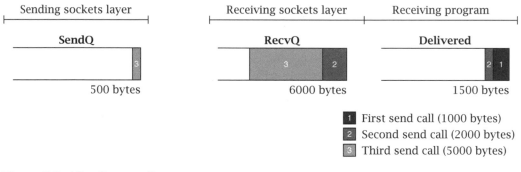

Figure 6.3: After first recv().

controlled or directly observed by the user program and that it occurs in chunks whose sizes are more or less independent of the size of the buffers passed in send() calls. Bytes are moved from **RecvQ** to **Delivered** as a result of recv() calls by the receiving program. The size of the transferred chunks depends on the amount of data in **RecvQ** and the size of the buffer given to recv().

Figure 6.2 shows one possible state of the three queues *after* the three send()s in the example above but *before* any recv()s at the other end. The different shadings denote bytes passed in the three different calls to send() shown above.

Now suppose the receiver calls recv() and gives it a buffer size of 2000 (bytes). The recv() call will return all of the 1500 bytes present in the waiting-for-delivery (**RecvQ**) queue. Note that this number includes data from the first and second calls to send(). At some time later, after TCP has completed transfer of more data, the three partitions would be as shown in Figure 6.3.

If the receiver now calls recv() with a buffer size of 4000, that many bytes will be moved from the waiting-for-delivery (**RecvQ**) queue to the already-delivered (**Delivered**) queue. This

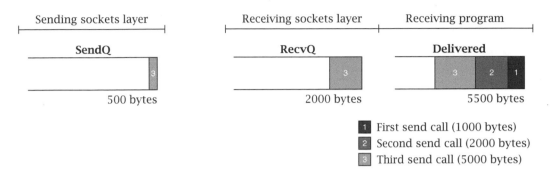

Figure 6.4: After another recv().

number includes the remaining 1500 bytes from the second send(), plus the first 2500 bytes from the third send(). The resulting state of the queues is shown in Figure 6.4. The number of bytes returned by the next call to recv() depends on the size of the buffer and the timing with respect to the transfer of data from the send-side queue to the receive-side queue.

The movement of data from the **SendQ** to the **RecvQ** buffer has important implications for the design of application protocols. We have already encountered the need to parse messages as they are received over a TCP socket when in-band delimiters are used for framing (Section 3.4). In the following sections, we consider two more subtle ramifications.

6.2 Deadlock

The buffers **SendQ** and **RecvQ** in the implementation are limited in their capacity. Although the actual amount of memory they use may grow and shrink dynamically, a hard limit is necessary to prevent all the system's memory from being gobbled up by a single TCP connection under control of a misbehaving program. These limits can be changed, as we saw in Section 5.1. The SO_SNDBUF option controls the size of **SendQ**, and SO_RCVBUF controls the size of **RecvQ**. The point is that these buffers are finite and, therefore, they can fill up. Let's consider some of the implications of that fact.

Once **RecvQ** is full, the TCP *flow control* mechanism kicks in and prevents the transfer of any bytes from the sending host's **SendQ** until space becomes available in **RecvQ** (as a result of a call to recv()). A sending program can continue to call send() until **SendQ** is full. Once **SendQ** is full, send() blocks until space becomes available, that is, until some bytes are transferred to the receiving host's **RecvQ**. If **RecvQ** is also full, everything stops until the receiving program calls recv(), so that some bytes can be transferred to **Delivered**.

Let's assume the sizes of **SendQ** and **RecvQ** are **SQS** and **RQS**, respectively. Assuming default (blocking) semantics, a send() call with a size parameter n such that $n > $ **SQS** will not return until at least $n - $ **SQS** bytes have been transferred to **RecvQ** at the receiving host. If the parameter n exceeds **SQS** + **RQS**, send() cannot return until after the receiving program has

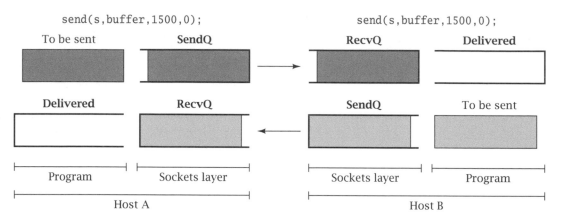

Figure 6.5: Deadlock caused by simultaneous send()s.

called recv() enough times or with a big enough buffer to allow at least $n - (\mathbf{SQS} + \mathbf{RQS})$ bytes of data to be delivered. If the receiving program does not call recv(), a large send() may not complete successfully. In particular, if both ends of the connection call send() simultaneously with size parameters greater than $\mathbf{SQS} + \mathbf{RQS}$, deadlock will result: Neither send() will ever complete, and both programs will remain blocked forever.

One way this can happen is if both programs are sending simultaneously. As a concrete example, consider a connection between a program on Host A and a program on Host B. Assume **SQS** and **RQS** are 500 at both A and B. Figure 6.5 shows what happens when both programs try to send() 1500 bytes at the same time. The first 500 bytes of data at Host A have been transferred to the other end; another 500 bytes have been copied into **SendQ** at Host A. The remaining 500 bytes cannot be sent—and, therefore, send() will not return—until space frees up in **RecvQ** at Host B. Unfortunately, the same situation holds for the program at Host B. Therefore, neither program's send() call will ever complete. The moral of the story: Design the protocol carefully to avoid simultaneous send()s in both directions.

6.3 Performance Implications

The need to copy user data into **SendQ** for potential retransmission also has implications for performance. In particular, the sizes of the **SendQ** and **RecvQ** buffers affect the *throughput* achievable over a TCP connection. *Throughput* refers to the rate at which bytes of user data from the sender are made available to the receiving program. In programs that transfer a large amount of data, we want to maximize this rate. In the absence of network capacity or other limitations, bigger buffers generally result in higher throughput.

The reason for this has to do with the cost of transferring data into or out of the kernel buffers. If you want to transfer n bytes of data (where $n \gg 1$), it is much more efficient to call send() once, with size parameter n, than it is to call it n times with size parameter 1.[2] However, if you call send() with a size parameter that is much larger than **SQS**, the system has to transfer the data from the user address space in **SQS**-sized chunks. That is, the socket layer fills up the **SendQ** buffer, waits for data to be transferred out of it by the TCP protocol, refills **SendQ**, waits some more, and so on. Each time the sockets layer has to wait for data to be removed from **SendQ**, some time is wasted in the form of overhead (i.e., a context switch occurs). This overhead is approximately the same as that incurred by a completely new system call. Thus, the *effective* size of a call to send() is limited by the actual **SQS**. For receive, the same principle applies: However large the buffer you give to recv(), it will be copied out in chunks no larger than **RQS**, with overhead incurred between chunks.

If you are writing a program for which throughput is an important performance metric, you will probably want to change the send and receive buffer sizes using the SO_RCVBUF and SO_SNDBUF socket options. Although there is always a system-imposed maximum size for each buffer, it is typically significantly larger than the default on modern systems. Remember that these considerations apply only if your program needs to send an amount of data significantly larger than the buffer size all at once.

6.4 TCP Socket Life Cycle

The sockets interface permits send() and recv() on a TCP socket only when it is in the connected or "Established" state, that is, only when it has completed the opening handshake message exchange required to establish a TCP connection. Let us now consider how a socket gets to and from the Established state; as we'll see in Section 6.4.2, these details affect the definition of reliability and the behavior of bind(). In what follows, as in all the examples of this book, we assume that connect() is called by the client and that the server calls bind(), listen(), and accept().

6.4.1 Connecting

The relationship between the connect() call and the protocol events associated with connection establishment at the client is illustrated in Figure 6.6. In this and the remaining figures of this section, the large arrows depict events that cause the socket structures to change state. Events that occur in the application program (i.e., function calls and returns) are shown in the upper part of the figure; events such as message arrivals are shown in the lower part of the figure. Time proceeds left to right in these figures. The client's Internet address is depicted as A.B.C.D, and the server's is W.X.Y.Z; the server's port number is Q.

---

[2] The same thing generally applies to recv(), although calling recv() with a larger buffer size parameter does not guarantee that more data will be returned (unless you change the socket semantics—compare the MSG_WAITALL flag).

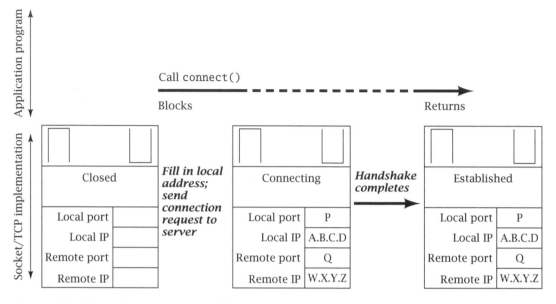

Figure 6.6: Client-side connection establishment.

When the client creates a TCP socket, it is initially in the Closed state. When the client calls connect() with Internet address W.X.Y.Z and port Q, the system fills in the four address fields in the socket structure. Because the client did not previously call bind(), a local port number (P), not already in use by another TCP socket, is chosen by the system and assigned to this socket. The local Internet address is also assigned; the address used is that of the network interface through which packets will be sent to the server (A.B.C.D).

The TCP opening handshake is known as a "three-way" handshake because it typically involves three messages: a connection request from client to server, an acknowledgment from server to client, and another acknowledgment from the client back to the server. The client TCP considers the connection to be established as soon as it receives the acknowledgment from the server. If the client TCP does not receive a response from the server within a reasonable period of time, it *times out* and gives up. In this case the connect() returns −1, with errno set to ETIMEDOUT. (The protocol retransmits handshake messages multiple times, at increasing intervals, before giving up. Thus, it can take on the order of minutes for a connect() call to fail.) If the server is not accepting connections—say, if there is no socket bound to the given port at the destination—the server-side TCP will send a rejection message instead of an acknowledgment, and connect() returns −1 (almost immediately) with errno set to ECONNREFUSED.

The sequence of events at the server side is rather different; we describe it in three Figures: 6.7, 6.8, and 6.9. The server needs to bind to the particular TCP port known to the client. Typically, the server specifies only the port number (here, Q) in the bind() call and

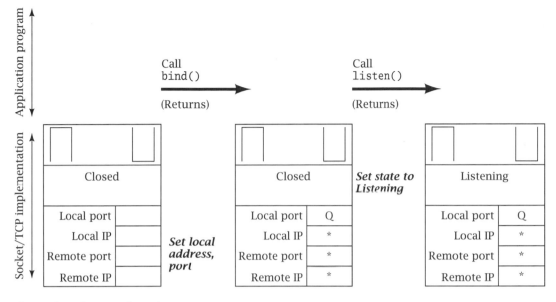

Figure 6.7: Server-side socket setup.

gives the special wildcard address INADDR_ANY for the local IP address. In case the server host has more than one IP address, this technique allows the socket to receive connections addressed to any of its IP addresses. When the server calls listen(), the state of the socket is changed to Listening, indicating that it is ready to accept new connections. These events are depicted in Figure 6.7. Note that any client connection request that arrives at the server before the call to listen() will be rejected, even if it arrives after the call to bind().

The next thing the server does is call accept(), which blocks until a connection with a client is established. We therefore focus in Figure 6.8 on the events that occur in the TCP implementation when a client connection request arrives. Note that everything depicted in this figure happens "under the covers," in the TCP implementation.

When the request for a connection arrives from the client, a new socket structure is created for the connection. The new socket's addresses are filled in based on the arriving packet: The packet's destination Internet address and port (W.X.Y.Z and Q, respectively) become the socket's local address and port; the packet's source address and port (A.B.C.D and P) become the socket's remote Internet address and port. Note that the local port number of the new socket is always the same as that of the listening socket. The new socket's state is set to Connecting, and it is added to a list of not-quite-connected sockets associated with the original server socket. Note well that the original server socket does not change state.

In addition to creating the new socket structure, the server-side TCP implementation sends an acknowledging TCP handshake message back to the client. However, the server TCP does not consider the handshake complete until the third message of the three-way handshake

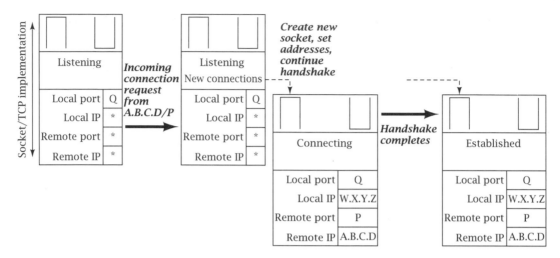

Figure 6.8: Incoming connection request processing.

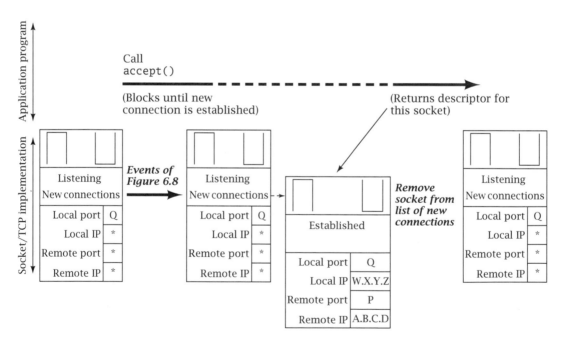

Figure 6.9: accept() processing.

is received from the client. When that message eventually arrives, the new socket's state is set to Established, and it is ready to be accept()ed.

Now we can consider what happens when the server program calls accept() on the listening socket (see Figure 6.9). The call unblocks as soon as there is something in the listening socket's list of new connections. At that time, the new socket structure is removed from the list, and a socket descriptor is allocated and returned as the result of accept().

6.4.2 Closing a TCP Connection

TCP has a *graceful close* mechanism that allows applications to terminate a connection without having to worry about loss of data that might still be in transit. The mechanism is also designed to allow data transfer in each direction to be terminated independently, although none of our examples so far have exhibited this capability. It works like this: The application indicates that it is finished sending data on a connected socket by calling close() or by calling shutdown() with second argument greater than zero. At that point, the underlying TCP implementation first transmits any data remaining in **SendQ** (subject to available space in **RecvQ** at the other end) and then sends a closing TCP handshake message to the other end. This closing handshake message can be thought of as an end-of-transmission marker; it tells the other TCP that no more bytes will be placed in **RecvQ**. The closing TCP waits for an acknowledgment of its closing handshake message, which indicates that all data sent on the connection safely made it to **RecvQ**. The connection at this point is "half-closed." It is not completely closed until a symmetric handshake happens in the other direction, that is, until both ends have indicated that they have no more data to send.

The closing event sequence in TCP can happen in two ways: Either one application calls close() and completes its close handshake before the other calls close(), or both call close() more or less simultaneously, so that their close handshake messages cross in the network. Figure 6.10 shows the sequence of events when one application calls close() before the other end closes. The closing handshake message is sent, the descriptor is deallocated, the state is set to Closing, and the call returns. When the acknowledgment for the close handshake is received, the state changes to Half-Closed, where it remains until the other end's close handshake message is received. (If the remote endpoint goes away while the socket is in this state, the socket structure will stay around indefinitely.) When the other end's close handshake message arrives, an acknowledgment is sent, and the state is changed to Time-Wait. Although the descriptor in the application program has long since vanished, the socket structure continues to exist in the socket/TCP implementation for a minute or more; the reasons for this are discussed below.

Figure 6.11 shows the simpler sequence of events at the endpoint that does not close first. When the closing handshake message arrives, an acknowledgment is sent immediately, and the connection state becomes Close-Wait. At this point, it is just waiting for the application to call close(). When close() is called, the descriptor for the socket is deallocated and the final close handshake initiated. When it completes, the entire socket structure is deallocated.

Although most applications use close(), shutdown() actually provides more flexibility. A call to close() terminates *both* directions of transfer and causes the file descriptor associated

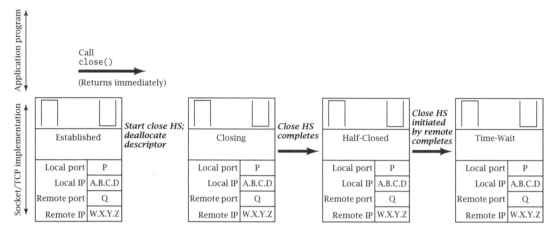

Figure 6.10: Closing a TCP connection first.

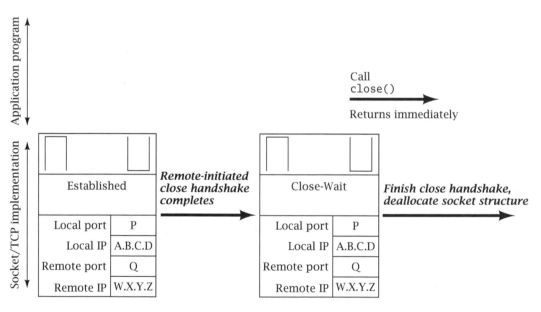

Figure 6.11: Closing after the other end closes.

with the socket to be deallocated. Any undelivered data remaining in **RecvQ** is discarded, and the flow control mechanism prevents any further transfer of data from the other end's **SendQ**. All trace of the socket disappears from the calling program. Underneath, however, the socket structure continues to exist until the other end initiates its closing handshake.

---

int shutdown(**int** *socket*, **int** *direction*)

---

shutdown() controls the closing of the connection of *socket*. *direction* specifies the part of the connection to close. If *direction* is 0, no further receives are allowed. If *direction* is 1, no further sends are allowed. If *direction* is 2, no further sends or receives are allowed. Often the constants SHUT_RD, SHUT_WR, and SHUT_RDWR are defined for 0, 1, and 2, respectively.

A program calling shutdown() with second argument SHUT_WR can continue to receive data on the socket; only sending is prohibited. The fact that the other end of the connection has closed is indicated by recv() returning 0 (once **RecvQ** is empty, of course) to indicate that there will be no more data available on the connection.

In view of the fact that both close() and shutdown() return without waiting for the closing handshake to complete, you may wonder how the sender can be assured that sent data has actually made it to the receiving program (i.e., to **Delivered**). In fact, it is possible for an application to call close() or shutdown() and have it return 0 (no error) *while there is still data in* **SendQ**. If either end of the connection then crashes before the data makes it to **RecvQ**, data may be lost without the sending application knowing about it.

There are two possible solutions. One is to design the application protocol so that the side that calls close() first does so only after receiving application-level assurance that its data was received. For example, when our program TCPEchoClient.c (page 13) receives the echoed copy of its data, there should be nothing more in transit in either direction, and therefore it is safe to close the connection.

The other solution is to modify the semantics of close() by setting the SO_LINGER socket option before calling it. The SO_LINGER option specifies an amount of time for the TCP implementation to wait for the closing handshake to complete. The setting of SO_LINGER and the specification of the wait time is given to setsockopt() using the **linger** structure:

```
struct linger {
    int  l_onoff;  /* Nonzero to linger */
    int  l_linger; /* Time (secs.) to linger */
};
```

To use the linger behavior, set l_onoff to a nonzero value and specify the time to linger in l_linger. When SO_LINGER is set, close() blocks *until the closing handshake is completed* or until the specified amount of time passes. If the handshake does not complete in time, an error indication (ETIMEDOUT) is returned. Thus, if SO_LINGER is set and close() returns no error, the application is assured that everything it sent reached **RecvQ**.

The final subtlety of closing a TCP connection revolves around the need for the Time-Wait state. When a TCP connection terminates, at least one of the sockets involved is supposed to persist in the Time-Wait state for a period of anywhere from 30 seconds to 2 minutes after both closing handshakes complete. This requirement is motivated by the possibility of messages being delayed in the network. If both endpoints' data structures go away as soon as both closing handshakes complete, and a *new* connection is immediately established between the same pair of socket addresses, a message from the previous connection, which happened to be delayed in the network, could arrive just after the new instance is established. Because it would contain the same source and destination addresses, it would be mistaken for a message belonging to the new instance, and its data might (incorrectly) be delivered as though it were part of the new connection.

Unlikely though this scenario may be, TCP employs multiple mechanisms to prevent it, including the Time-Wait state. The purpose of the Time-Wait state is to ensure that every TCP connection ends with a "quiet time," during which no data is sent. The quiet time is supposed to be equal to twice the maximum amount of time a packet can remain in the network. Thus, by the time a connection goes away completely (i.e., by the time the socket structure leaves the Time-Wait state and is deallocated) and clears the way for a new instance, no messages from the old instance can still be in the network. In practice, the length of the quiet time is implementation dependent, because there is no real mechanism that limits how long a packet can be delayed by the network. Values in use range from 4 minutes down to 30 seconds or even shorter.

As long as one of the two sockets involved in a connection persists, any attempt to establish a new instance will fail, because the connect request message will be delivered to the socket belonging to the old instance at one end or the other (see Section 6.5), resulting in rejection of the connect request. The most important consequence of Time-Wait is that as long as the socket exists, no other socket is permitted to bind() to the same local port (bind() returns EADDRINUSE in that case).

6.5 Demultiplexing Demystified

The fact that different sockets on the same machine can have the same local address and port number is implicit in the discussions above. For example, on a machine with only one IP address, every new socket accept()ed via a listening socket will have the same local address and port number as the listening socket. Clearly, the process of deciding to which socket an incoming packet should be delivered—that is, the *demultiplexing* process—involves looking at more than just the packet's destination address and port. Otherwise, there could be ambiguity about which socket an incoming packet is intended for. The process of matching an incoming packet to a socket is actually the same for both TCP and UDP and can be summarized by the following points:

- The local port in the socket structure must match the destination port number in the incoming packet exactly.

- Any address fields in the socket structure that contain the wildcard value ("*") are considered to match *any* value in the corresponding field in the packet.

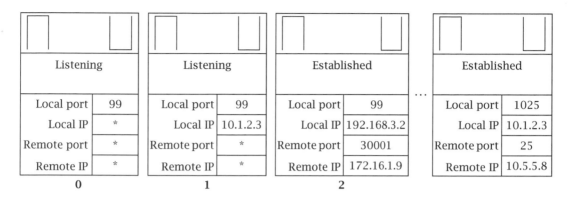

Figure 6.12: Demultiplexing with multiple matching sockets.

- If there is more than one socket that matches an incoming packet for all fields, the one that matched using the fewest wildcards gets the packet.

For example, consider a host with two IP addresses, 10.1.2.3 and 192.168.3.2, and with part of its list of active TCP sockets as shown in Figure 6.12. Socket 0 is bound to port 99 with a wildcard local address, Socket 1 is a listening socket on the same port that will accept only connections to 10.1.2.3, and Socket 2 belongs to a connection that was accepted via Socket 0, and thus has the same local port number but also has its local Internet address and remote addresses filled in. Other sockets belong to other active connections. Now consider a packet with source IP address 172.16.1.10, source port 56789, destination IP address 10.1.2.3, and destination port 99. It will be delivered to Socket 1 because that one matches with the fewest wildcards.

When a program attempts to bind() to a particular port number, the existing sockets are checked to make sure that no socket is already bound to that port. The call to bind() will fail and set EADDRINUSE if *any* socket matches the local port and IP address (if specified) given to bind(). This can cause problems in the following scenario:

1. A server's listening socket is bound to well-known port P.

2. A connection is accept()ed on that socket, and the server sends and receives on it.

3. The server program exits, so that a new version of the server can be started up, for example. Before terminating, it closes both the TCP connection and the listening socket. The TCP connection socket goes into the Time-Wait state.

4. A new instance of the server is immediately started up and attempts to bind() to well-known port P.

Unfortunately, the new server's bind() attempt will fail with EADDRINUSE because of the socket in Time-Wait state.

One way around this (that is, besides waiting until the quiet time is over to restart the server) is for the server to set the SO_REUSEADDR socket option, which enables multiple sockets to be bound to the same address *before* calling bind(). This option lets the bind() succeed in spite of the existence of any sockets representing earlier connections to the server's port. There is no danger of ambiguity, because the existing connections (whether still in the Established or Time-Wait state) have remote addresses filled in, while the socket being bound does not. In general, the SO_REUSEADDR option also enables a socket to bind to a local port to which another socket is already bound, provided that the IP address to which it is being bound (typically the wildcard INADDR_ANY address) is different from the existing socket's. The default bind() behavior is to disallow such requests.

Thought Questions

1. The TCP protocol is designed so that simultaneous connection attempts will succeed. That is, if an application using port P and Internet address W.X.Y.Z attempts to connect to address A.B.C.D, port Q, at the same time as the latter tries to connect to W.X.Y.Z port P, they will end up connected to each other. Can this be made to happen when the programs use the sockets API?

2. The deadlock example in this chapter involves the programs on both ends of a connection trying to send large messages. However, this is not necessary for deadlock. Modify the TCP echo client from Chapter 2 so that it deadlocks when it connects to the TCP echo server from that chapter.

chapter 7

Domain Name Service

The TCP/IP protocol family uses numeric Internet addresses (e.g., 169.1.1.1) and numeric ports (e.g., 5000) to describe communication endpoints. This makes the protocol implementations efficient but has at least two drawbacks. First, strings of numbers do not mean much to humans and are therefore hard for us to remember. And second, a host's Internet address is tied to the part of the network to which it is connected. This fosters inflexibility in their use. If a host moves to another network or changes Internet service providers (ISPs), in general, its Internet address must change.

To solve these problems, most implementations of the sockets API provide access to a *name service* that maps names to other information, including Internet addresses. For example, the Web server for the publisher of this text, Morgan Kaufmann, has an Internet address of 208.164.121.48; however, we refer to that Web server as www.mkp.com. Obviously, www.mkp.com is much easier to remember than 208.164.121.48. In fact, most likely this is how you typically think of specifying a host on the Internet: by name. In addition, if Morgan Kaufmann's Web server changes its Internet address for some reason (e.g., new ISP, server moves to another machine), simply changing the mapping of www.mkp.com from 208.164.121.48 to the new Internet address allows the change to be invisible to programs that use the name to access the Web server.

It is critical to remember that a naming service is not required for TCP/IP to work. Names simply provide a level of indirection, for the reasons discussed above. The host naming service can access information from a wide variety of sources. Two of the primary sources are the *Domain Name System* (DNS) and local configuration databases. The DNS [8] is a distributed database that maps *domain names* such as "www.mkp.com" to Internet addresses and other information; the DNS protocol [9] allows hosts connected to the Internet to retrieve information from that database using TCP or UDP. Local configuration databases are generally operating-system–specific mechanisms for name-to-Internet-address mappings.

7.1 Mapping Between Names and Internet Addresses

The function gethostbyname() takes the name of a host and returns the available host information from the naming service, including the host's Internet address. The source of the information is implementation dependent and may be the DNS, a local configuration database, or some combination of the two.

---

struct hostent *gethostbyname(**const char** *hostName*)

---

gethostbyname() either returns a **hostent** structure or NULL (error). The **hostent** structure contains relevant information about the host:

```
struct hostent {
    char *h_name;          /* Official name of host */
    char **h_aliases;      /* List of alias names (strings) */
    int h_addrtype;        /* Type of host address (AF_INET) */
    int h_length;          /* Address length */
    char **h_addr_list;    /* List of addresses (binary in network byte order) */
};
```

h_name is simply a string containing the official name of the host. Hosts can go by many names; however, one name is usually defined to be the official ("canonical") name. h_aliases is a pointer to an array of pointers to character arrays containing the other (alias) names of the host. h_addrtype gives the type of host address. For now, this should always be AF_INET. However, when (if) IPv6 becomes reality, AF_INET6 will also be a possible value. h_addr_list contains a list of the Internet addresses associated with the official name implemented as a pointer to an array of pointers; each element of the array points to an Internet address, in network byte order, independent of the architecture of the local host. h_length contains the length (bytes) of the addresses in h_addr_list. Since Internet addresses are 32 bits in length, this value is always 4. On error, gethostbyname() assigns the error number for *h_errno* (not *errno* as in previous socket function calls).

When given an Internet address instead of a host name, gethostbyname() returns a **hostent** structure with the given Internet address as the only item in the h_addr_list. This means that when given a host (whether a name or an Internet address) from the command line, we can simply call gethostbyname() and receive a correct **hostent** structure. The following code segment defines the function ResolveName(), which returns a binary, network-byte-ordered Internet address.

ResolveName()

```
0  #include <stdio.h>        /* for fprintf() */
1  #include <netdb.h>        /* for gethostbyname() */
2
```

```
 3  unsigned long ResolveName(char name[])
 4  {
 5      struct hostent *host;           /* Structure containing host information */
 6
 7      if ((host = gethostbyname(name)) == NULL)
 8      {
 9          fprintf(stderr, "gethostbyname() failed");
10          exit(1);
11      }
12
13      /* return the binary, network-byte-ordered address */
14      return *((unsigned long *) host->h_addr_list[0]);
15  }
```

ResolveName()

To use this in TCPEchoClient.c (page 13), replace

```
        echoServAddr.sin_addr.s_addr = inet_addr(servIP);   /* Server Internet address */
```

with

```
        echoServAddr.sin_addr.s_addr = ResolveName(servIP); /* Server address (name or IP) */
```

ResolveName() takes an address in either the name or dotted-quad representation and passes the string to gethostbyname(). If the address is valid, it takes the first element of the resulting h_addr_list—the binary address in network byte order—and returns it. If the name cannot be resolved and the parameter is not a valid, dotted-quad address, ResolveName() reports an error and exits.

So we can get an Internet address from a host name, but can we perform the inverse (host name from an Internet address)? gethostbyaddr() does exactly what we need. It takes the specification of an address in binary, network-byte-ordered representation and returns the available host information from the name service, which includes the host's official name and aliases.

struct hostent *gethostbyaddr(**const char** *address, **int** addressLength, **int** addressFamily)

Given a host address (pointer to binary, network-byte-ordered address), the length of the address (4), and the address family (AF_INET), gethostbyaddr() either returns a **hostent** structure (described previously) or NULL (error). As with gethostbyname(), the source of the information is unspecified—it may be a local database or the global DNS.

What if your program needs its own host's name? gethostname() takes a buffer and buffer length and copies the name of the host on which the calling program is running into the given buffer. One way for an application to get the Internet address of the machine on which it is running is to call gethostname() and then call ResolveName().

---

int gethostname(**char** **nameBuffer*, **size_t** *bufferLength*)

7.2   Finding Service Information by Name

By analogy with host names, the sockets API provides a way to obtain information about an application (server), including the port number it uses, by name. The function getservbyname() takes a service name (e.g., "echo") and the protocol ("tcp" or "udp") used by the server and returns the service information in a **servent** structure.

---

struct servent **getservbyname(**const char** **serviceName*, **const char** **protocol*)

---

getservbyname() either returns a **servent** structure or NULL (error). The **servent** structure contains relevant information about the service:

```
struct servent {
    char *s_name;        /* Official service name */
    char **s_aliases;    /* List of alternate names (strings) */
    int s_port;          /* Service port number */
    char *s_proto;       /* Implementation protocol ("tcp" or "udp") */
};
```

The **servent** structure is very similar to the **hostent** structure. s_name is a string containing the official name of the service. s_aliases provides the list of alternate names as a pointer to an array of pointers to character arrays containing these other names. s_port is the port of the service. s_proto gives the name of the protocol implementing this service (either "tcp" or "udp"). getservbyname() returns 0 for success and −1 otherwise.

Perhaps because there is less need for the additional level of indirection, there is no global database that maps names to port numbers. In UNIX, the information returned by getservbyname() usually comes from a local database or the /etc/services file. It is important to realize that the information returned by getservbyname() may not be valid for a host that is managed by a different administration; however, it is arguably better than nothing.

We demonstrate the use of getservbyname() in the function ResolveService(), which returns a binary, network-byte-ordered port given a service name or port number.

ResolveService()

```
0  #include <stdio.h>      /* for printf() and fprintf() */
1  #include <netinet/in.h> /* for htons() */
```

```
2   #include <netdb.h>        /* for getservbyname() */
3   #include <stdlib.h>       /* for atoi() */
4
5   unsigned short ResolveService(char service[], char protocol[])
6   {
7       struct servent *serv;        /* Structure containing service information */
8       unsigned short port;         /* Port to return */
9
10      if ((port = atoi(service)) == 0)  /* Is port numeric? */
11      {
12          /* Not numeric.  Try to find as name */
13          if ((serv = getservbyname(service, protocol)) == NULL)
14          {
15              fprintf(stderr, "getservbyname() failed");
16              exit(1);
17          }
18          else
19              port = serv->s_port;   /* Found port (network byte order) by name */
20      }
21      else
22          port = htons(port);  /* Convert port to network byte order */
23
24      return port;
25  }
```

ResolveService()

To use this function in TCPEchoClient.c (page 13), replace the port specification code

```
if (argc == 4)
    echoServPort = atoi(argv[3]); /* Use given port, if any */
else
    echoServPort = 7;  /* otherwise, 7 is the well-known port for the echo service */
```

with

```
char *cmdPort;                /* Port to send echo requests to */
    .
    .
    .
if (argc == 4)
    cmdPort = argv[3];        /* Use given port, if any */
else
    cmdPort = "echo";        /* otherwise, find echo service */
    .
    .
    .
echoServAddr.sin_port = ResolveService(cmdPort, "tcp"); /* Server port */
```

ResolveService() takes a service specification in the form of a port or service name and the service protocol. The function first attempts to convert the port from a string to an unsigned short using atoi(). Recall that 0 is a reserved port, so the port of a service should never be 0, and note that atoi() returns 0 if its argument cannot be converted to an integer. If atoi() returns a number other than 0, the return value is converted to network byte order by htons() and returned. If atoi() returns 0, ResolveService() assumes the service specification is a name and passes that name to getservbyname(). If the name is valid, getservbyname() returns a pointer to a **servent** structure where s_port contains the port already in network byte order. If getservbyname() returns NULL, the implementation does not know any service for the given name, so ResolveService() reports an error and exits.

getservbyport() goes the other direction. It takes a port number and the protocol implementing the service and returns the service information including the service name.

---

struct servent *getservbyport(**int** *port*, **const char** **protocol*)

Given the port (in network byte order) and the protocol, getservbyport() either returns a **servent** structure (described previously) or NULL (error).

PART 2

API REFERENCE

API Reference

Data Structures

- sockaddr

Generic (non–address-family-specific) address structure

```
#include <sys/socket.h>        /* Generic socket header file */

struct sockaddr
{
    unsigned short sa_family;  /* Address family (e.g., AF_INET) */
    char sa_data[14];          /* Protocol-specific address information */
};
```

- sockaddr_in

Internet protocol address structure

```
#include <netinet/in.h>     /* Internet protocol socket specifics */

struct in_addr
{
    unsigned long s_addr;      /* IP address (32 bits) */
};

struct sockaddr_in
{
    unsigned short sin_family; /* Internet protocol (AF_INET) */
    unsigned short sin_port;   /* Address port (16 bits) */
```

```
        struct in_addr sin_addr;   /* IP address (32 bits) */
        char sin_zero[8];          /* Not used */
    };
```

All values must be in network byte order (see Section 3.2). See TCPEchoClient.c (page 13) for usage example.

Socket Setup

• socket()

Creates a TCP or UDP socket, which may then be used as an endpoint of communication for sending and receiving data using the specified protocol. Specify TCP and UDP with socket type/protocol pair SOCK_STREAM/IPPROTO_TCP and SOCK_DGRAM/IPPROTO_UDP, respectively.

```
#include <sys/types.h>
#include <sys/socket.h>
```

int socket(**int** *protocolFamily*, **int** *type*, **int** *protocol*)

protocolFamily	Always PF_INET for TCP/IP sockets
type	Type of socket (SOCK_STREAM or SOCK_DGRAM)
protocol	Socket protocol (IPPROTO_TCP or IPPROTO_UDP)

socket() returns the descriptor of the new socket if no error occurs and −1 otherwise.

See TCPEchoServer.c (page 19) for usage example.

• bind()

Assigns the local Internet address and port for a socket. The port number must be specified. The call will fail (EADDRINUSE) if the specified port number is the local port of some other socket and the SO_REUSEADDR socket option has not been set.

```
#include <sys/types.h>
#include <sys/socket.h>
```
int bind(**int** *socket*, **struct sockaddr** **localAddress*, **unsigned int** *addressLength*)

socket	Socket (returned by socket())
localAddress	Populated **sockaddr** structure describing local address
addressLength	Number of bytes in **sockaddr** structure—usually just sizeof(*localAddress*)

bind() returns 0 if no error occurs and −1 otherwise.

See TCPEchoServer.c (page 19) for usage example.

• getsockname()

Returns the local information for a socket in a **sockaddr** structure.

```
#include <sys/socket.h>
int getsockname(int socket, struct sockaddr *localAddress,
                unsigned int *addressLength)
```

socket	Socket (returned by socket())
localAddress	**sockaddr** structure to return the local address
addressLength	In-out variable containing the number of bytes in **sockaddr** structure

getsockname() returns 0 if no error occurs and −1 otherwise.

Socket Connection

• connect()

Establishes a connection between the given socket and the remote socket associated with the foreign address, if any. Upon returning successfully, the given socket's local and remote IP address and port information are filled in. If the socket was not previously bound to a local port, one is assigned randomly. For TCP sockets, connect() returns successfully only after completing a handshake with the remote TCP implementation; success implies the existence of a reliable channel to that socket.

```
#include <sys/types.h>
#include <sys/socket.h>
int connect(int socket, struct sockaddr *foreignAddress, int addressLength)
```

socket	Socket (returned from socket())
foreignAddress	Populated **sockaddr** structure describing foreign socket address
addressLength	Number of bytes in **sockaddr** structure—usually just sizeof(*foreignAddress*)

connect() returns 0 if no error occurs and −1 otherwise.

See TCPEchoClient.c (page 13) for usage example.

- listen() (Stream/TCP sockets only)

Indicates that the given socket is ready to accept incoming connections. The socket must already be associated with a local port (i.e., bind() must have been called previously). After this call, incoming TCP connection requests addressed to the given local port (and IP address, if specified previously) will be completed and queued until they are passed to the program via accept().

```
#include <sys/types.h>
#include <sys/socket.h>
int listen(int socket, int backlog)
```

      socket   Socket (returned from socket())

      backlog   Maximum number of new connections (sockets) waiting

listen() returns 0 if no error occurs and −1 otherwise.

See TCPEchoServer.c (page 19) for usage example.

- accept() (Stream/TCP sockets only)

Blocks waiting for connections addressed to the IP address and port to which the given socket is bound. (listen() must previously have been called on the given socket.) When a connection arrives and the TCP handshake is successfully completed, a new socket is returned. The local and remote address and port numbers of the new socket have been filled in with the local port number of the new socket, and the address information has been returned in the **sockaddr_in** structure.

```
#include <sys/types.h>
#include <sys/socket.h>
int accept(int socket, struct sockaddr *clientAddress, int *addressLength)
```

      socket   Socket (listen() already called)

      clientAddress   Originating socket IP address and port

      addressLength Length of **sockaddr** buffer (in), returned address (out)

accept() returns the newly connected socket descriptor if no error occurs and −1 otherwise.

See TCPEchoServer.c (page 19) for usage example. See Section 6.4.1 for details.

- getpeername()

Returns the remote information for a socket in a **sockaddr** structure.

```
#include <sys/socket.h>
```

int getpeername(**int** *socket*, **struct sockaddr** **localAddress*, **unsigned int** **addressLength*)

socket	Socket (returned by socket())
localAddress	**sockaddr** structure to return the remote address
addressLength	In-out variable containing the number of bytes in **sockaddr** structure

getpeername() returns 0 if no error occurs and −1 otherwise.

Socket Communication

* send()
_____

Sends the bytes contained in the buffer over the given socket. The socket must be in a connected state. When the call returns, the data has been queued for transmission over the connection. Semantics depends on the type of socket. For a stream socket, the data will eventually be transmitted, provided the connection closes normally. For a datagram socket, there are no guarantees of delivery. However, the data from a single send() call will never be split across multiple recv() calls. The return value indicates the number of bytes actually transmitted. The *flags* argument allows various special protocol features, such as out-of-band data, to be accessed.

```
#include <sys/types.h>
#include <sys/socket.h>
int send(int socket, const void *msg, unsigned int msgLength, int flags)
```

socket	Socket (must be in connected state)
msg	Pointer to data to be transmitted
msgLength	Number of bytes to be sent
flags	Control flags (0 in most cases)

send() returns the number of bytes sent if no error occurs and −1 otherwise.

See TCPEchoClient.c (page 13) for usage example. See Section 6.1 for detailed TCP semantics.

* sendto()
_____

Sends the bytes contained in the buffer over the given socket. To use sendto() on a TCP socket requires the socket to be in the connected state. The semantics for sendto() are the same as the semantics of send().

```
#include <sys/types.h>
#include <sys/socket.h>
```

int sendto(**int** *socket,* **char** **msg,* **int** *msgLength,* **int** *flags,*
          struct sockaddr **destAddr,* **int** *destAddrLen)*

socket	Socket (must be in connected state)
msg	Pointer to data to be transmitted
msgLength	Number of bytes to be sent
flags	Control flags (0 in most cases)
destAddr	Destination address for data
destAddrLen	Length of destination address structure

sendto() returns the number of bytes sent if no error occurs and −1 otherwise.

See UDPEchoClient.c (page 36) for usage example.

• **recv()**

Copies up to a specified number of bytes, received on the socket, into a specified location.
The given socket must be in the connected state. Normally, the call blocks until either at least
one byte is returned or the connection closes. The return value indicates the number of bytes
actually copied into the buffer starting at the pointed-to location. Semantics depends on the
type of socket. For a stream socket, the bytes are delivered in the same order as they were
transmitted, without omissions. For a datagram socket, each recv() returns the data from at
most one send(), and order is not necessarily preserved. If the buffer provided to recv() is
not big enough for the next available datagram, the datagram is silently truncated to the size
of the buffer.

```
#include <sys/types.h>
#include <sys/socket.h>
int recvfrom(int socket, void *rcvBuffer, int bufferLength, int flags)
```

socket	Socket (must be in connected state)
rcvBuffer	Where to put the data
bufferLength	Maximum number of bytes to put in buffer
flags	Control flags, 0 in most cases

recv() returns the number of bytes received if no error occurs and −1 otherwise.

See TCPEchoClient.c (page 13) for usage example. See Section 6.1 for detailed semantics.

• **recvfrom()**

Copies up to a specified number of bytes, received on the socket, into a specified location. To
use recvfrom() on a TCP socket requires the socket to be in the connected state. The semantics
for recvfrom() are the same as the semantics of recv().

```
#include <sys/types.h>
#include <sys/socket.h>
int recvfrom(int socket, char *buffer, int bufferSize, int flags,
        struct sockaddr *fromAddr, unsigned int *fromAddrLen)
```

socket	Socket (must be in connected state)
buffer	Where to put the data
bufferSize	Max number of bytes to put in buffer
flags	Control flags (0 in most cases)
fromAddr	Address data of sender
fromAddrLen	Length of sender address structure

recv() returns the number of bytes received if no error occurs and −1 otherwise.

See UDPEchoClient.c (page 36) for usage example.

- close()

Terminates communication on a socket. The socket is marked to disallow further sends and receives.

```
#include <unistd.h>
int close(int socket)
```

socket	Socket (must be in connected state)

close() returns 0 if no error occurs and −1 otherwise.

See TCPEchoClient.c (page 13) for usage example.

- shutdown()

Terminates communication on a socket. The socket is marked to disallow further sends, receives, or both, according to the second parameter: If it is 0, further receives will be disallowed. If it is 1, further sends are disallowed. If it is 2, both sends and receives will be disallowed. The socket must be in the connected state.

```
#include <sys/socket.h>
int shutdown(int socket, int how)
```

socket	Socket (must be in connected state)
how	0 = done receiving, 1 = done sending, 2 = done sending and receiving

shutdown() returns 0 if no error occurs and −1 otherwise.

See page 99 for additional information.

Socket Control

• `getsockopt()`
_____

Retrieves an option on a socket. Socket options are used to alter the default socket behavior.

```
#include <sys/types.h>
#include <sys/socket.h>
int getsockopt(int socket, int level, int optName, void *optVal,
               unsigned int *optLen)
```

socket	Socket
level	Option level (see Section 5.1, page 43)
optName	Option name (see Section 5.1)
optVal	Pointer to buffer to record option value (see Table 5.1)
optLen	Length (bytes) of option value

getsockopt() returns 0 if no error occurs and −1 otherwise.

See Table 5.1 (page 45) and the code segment on page 44.

• `setsockopt()`
_____

Sets the options on a socket. Socket options are used to alter the default socket behavior.

```
#include <sys/types.h>
#include <sys/socket.h>
int setsockopt(int socket, int level, int optName, const void *optVal,
               unsigned int optLen)
```

socket	Socket
level	Option level (see Section 5.1, page 43)
optName	Option name (see Section 5.1)
optVal	Pointer to buffer holding option value (see Table 5.1)
optLen	Length (bytes) of option value buffer

setsockopt() returns 0 if no error occurs and −1 otherwise.

See Table 5.1 (page 45) and the code segment on page 44.

Binary/String Conversion

- `inet_ntoa()`

Converts an IP address in binary notation (network byte order) to the corresponding string in dotted notation (e.g., "169.1.1.2").

```
#include <sys/socket.h>
#include <netinet/in.h>
#include <arpa/inet.h>
char *inet_ntoa(struct in_addr address)
```

> *address*   Structure containing 32-bit representation of IP address

inet_ntoa() returns a pointer to a string. The string is a statically allocated buffer whose value changes with every call; therefore, the buffer should be copied before subsequent calls.

See TCPEchoServer.c (page 19) for usage example.

- `inet_addr()`

Converts an IP address in dotted notation to the corresponding binary notation (network byte order).

```
#include <sys/socket.h>
#include <netinet/in.h>
#include <arpa/inet.h>
char *inet_addr(const char *address)
```

> *address*   Pointer to character string containing dotted representation
> of IP address

inet_addr() returns the unsigned long, binary representation of the IP address if no error occurs and −1 otherwise.

See TCPEchoClient.c (page 13) for usage example.

- `htons(), htonl(), ntohs(), ntohl()`

Converts host to network byte order and vice versa.

```
#include <netinet/in.h>

short int htons(short int hostShort)
long int htonl(long int hostLong)
```

short int ntohs(**short int** *netShort*)
long int ntohl(**long int** *netLong*)

hostShort	Short integer in host byte order
hostLong	Long integer in host byte order
netShort	Short integer in network byte order
netLong	Long integer in network byte order

htons(), htonl(), ntohs(), and ntohl() return the converted value. These functions have no failure return value.

See TCPEchoClient.c (page 13) for usage example.

Host and Service Information

- gethostname()

---

gethostname() returns the local host name in the specified buffer.

int gethostname(**char** **hostName,* **unsigned int** *length*)

hostName	Buffer to hold the host name
length	Length of *hostName* buffer

gethostname() returns −1 for failure; 0 otherwise.

- gethostbyname()

Given the name of a host, gethostbyname() returns a **hostent** structure containing a description of the named host.

```
#include <netdb.h>
struct hostent *gethostbyname(const char *hostName)
```

hostName	Name of host to get information about

gethostbyname() returns NULL on error and a pointer to a **hostent** structure on success:

```
struct hostent {
    char *h_name;          /* Official name of host */
    char **h_aliases;      /* List of alias names (strings) */
    int h_addrtype;        /* Type of host address (AF_INET) */
    int h_length;          /* Address length */
    char **h_addr_list;    /* List of addresses (binary in network byte order) */
};
```

See Section 7.1 for description of **hostent** fields. If *hostName* is an IP address instead of a name, gethostbyname() copies the string to *h_name* and places an entry for the IP address (binary) in *h_addr_list*. See ResolveName() (page 104) for usage example.

• gethostbyaddr()

Given an IP address, gethostbyaddr() returns a **hostent** structure containing a description of the host with the given IP address.

```
#include <netdb.h>

#include <sys/socket.h>
struct hostent *gethostbyaddr(const char *address, int addressLength, int addressFamily)
```

address	Address (in binary, network-byte ordered representation) of host to get information about
addressLength	Length of given address (in bytes)
addressFamily	Family of given address (AF_INET)

gethostbyaddr() returns NULL on error and a **hostent** structure (see gethostbyname(), above) on success.

• getservbyname()

Given the name of a service (e.g., echo) and the protocol implementing that service, getservbyname() returns a **servent** structure containing a description of the named service.

```
#include <netdb.h>
struct servent *getservbyname(const char *serviceName, const char *protocol)
```

serviceName	Name of service to get information about
protocol	Name of protocol implementing the service ("tcp" or "udp")

getservbyname() returns NULL on error and a **servent** structure on success:

```
struct servent {
    char *s_name;         /* Official service name */
    char **s_aliases;     /* List of alias names (strings) */
    int h_addrtype;       /* Type of host address (AF_INET) */
    int h_length;         /* Address length */
    char **h_addr_list;   /* List of addresses (binary in network byte order) */
};
```

See Section 7.2 for description of **servent** fields. See ResolveService() (page 106) for usage example.

• `getservbyport()`

Given a port and the name of the service protocol, `getservbyport()` returns a **servent** structure containing a description of the service with the given port and protocol.

```
#include <netdb.h>

#include <sys/socket.h>
struct servent *getservbyport(int port, const char *protocol)
```

port	Port (in binary, network-byte-ordered representation) of service to get information about
protocol	Name of protocol implementing the service ("tcp" or "udp")

`getservbyport()` returns NULL on error and a **servent** structure (see `getservbyname()`, above) on success.

Bibliography

[1] Case, J. D., Fedor, M., and Schoffstall, M. L. "Simple Network Management Protocol (SNMP)." Internet Request for Comments 1157, May 1990.

[2] Comer, Douglas E. *Internetworking with TCP/IP*, volume 1, *Principles, Protocols, and Architecture* (third edition). Prentice Hall, 1995.

[3] Comer, Douglas E., and Stevens, David L. *Internetworking with TCP/IP*, volume 2, *Design, Implementation, and Internals* (third edition). Prentice Hall, 1999.

[4] Comer, Douglas E., and Stevens, David L. *Internetworking with TCP/IP*, volume 3, *Client-Server Programming and Applications* (BSD version, second edition). Prentice Hall, 1996.

[5] Deering, S., and Hinden, R. "Internet Protocol, Version 6 (IPv6) Specification." Internet Request for Comments 2460, December 1998.

[6] Gilligan, R., Thomson, S., Bound, J., and Stevens, W. "Basic Socket Interface Extensions for IPv6." Internet Request for Comments 2553, March 1999.

[7] International Organization for Standardization. *Basic Encoding Information Processing Systems: Open Systems Interconnection—Specification of Abstract Syntax Notation One (ASN.1)*. International Standard 8824, December 1987.

[8] Mockapetris, Paul. "Domain Names: Concepts and Facilities." Internet Request for Comments 1034, November 1987.

[9] Mockapetris, Paul. "Domain Names: Implementation and Specification." Internet Request for Comments 1035, November 1987.

[10] Peterson, Larry L., and Davie, Bruce S. *Computer Networks: A Systems Approach* (second edition). Morgan Kaufmann, 2000.

[11] Postel, John. "Internet Protocol." Internet Request for Comments 791, September 1981.

[12] Postel, John. "Transmission Control Protocol." Internet Request for Comments 793, September 1981.

[13] Postel, John. "User Datagram Protocol." Internet Request for Comments 768, August 1980.

[14] Steedman, Douglas. *Abstract Syntax Notation One (ASN.1): The Tutorial and Reference.* Technology Appraisals (U.K.), 1990.

[15] Stevens, W. Richard. *TCP/IP Illustrated,* volume 1, *The Protocols.* Addison-Wesley, 1994.

[16] Stevens, W. Richard. *UNIX Network Programming: Networking APIs: Sockets and XTI* (second edition). Prentice Hall, 1997.

[17] Sun Microsystems, Incorporated. "External Data Representation Standard." Internet Request for Comments 1014, June 1987.

[18] Sun Microsystems, Incorporated. "Network File System Protocol Specification." Internet Request for Comments 1094, March 1989.

[19] Sun Microsystems, Incorporated. "Network File System Protocol Version 3 Specification." Internet Request for Comments 1813, June 1995.

[20] Wright, Gary R., and Stevens, W. Richard. *TCP/IP Illustrated,* volume 2, *The Implementation.* Addison-Wesley, 1995.

Index

accept()
  API reference, 114
  blocking, 50
  demultiplexing and, 101
  local addresses and, 100
  multiple I/O channels and,
    72
  return values, 18
  select() for timeout
    implementation, 77
  server-side processing, 95-97
  syntax, 18
  TCP server setup, 17, 18
  in TCPEchoServer.c, 21
  in TCPEchoServer-Thread.c,
    69
  in UDPEchoServer.c, 41
AcceptTCPConnection(), 63
AcceptTCPConnection.c, 66
addresses. *See also* Internet
    addresses; port numbers;
    sockaddr; sockaddr_in
  client connection request
    processing, 95, 96
  demultiplexing, 100-102
  dotted-quad notation, 6
  overview, 5-6
  of sockets, 8
  specifying for sockets, 10-11
AF_INET6, 104
AF_INET
  with **hostent** structure, 104,
    105
  PF_INET vs., 11

with **sockaddr** structure,
    10
  TCPEchoClient.c and, 15
alarm(), 56
alarms, 56, 59, 77
alignment of message data,
    30-31
API reference, 109-122
  binary/string conversion,
    119-120
  data structures, 111-112
  host and service information,
    120-122
  socket communication,
    115-117
  socket connection, 113-115
  socket control, 118
  socket setup, 112-113
application protocols, 25
applications, 7
asynchronous I/O, 51-55
  overview, 51-52
  UDPEchoServer-SIGIO.c,
    52-55
atoi(), 108

bank example assumptions,
    25-26
Big-Endian architecture, 28-29
binary/string conversion,
    119-120
bind()
  API reference, 112-113
  demultiplexing, 101-102

listen() and, 114
  for local ports, 87
  return values, 18
  server call to, 93, 94-95
  syntax, 17
  TCP server setup, 17-18
  in TCPEchoServer.c, 20-21,
    22, 23
  Time-Wait state and, 100
blocking, 49, 50, 56
broadcast, 77-81
  described, 77
  directed, 77-78
  local, 77
  multicast vs., 85
  network-wide to all hosts,
    78
  receiver, 80-81
  sender, 78-79
  unicast vs., 77
BroadcastReceiver.c, 80-81
BroadcastSender.c, 78-79
buffering
  deadlock, 91-92
  performance implications,
    92-93
  TCP and, 89-91
byte ordering in messages,
    28-30
  Big-Endian architecture,
    28-29
  Little-Endian architecture,
    28-29
  network byte order, 29-30

CatchAlarm(), 59
character encoding, 26
child processes, 60, 63, 64, 72
clients
  client-side connection
    establishment, 93-94
  closing handshake, 97-100
  opening handshake, 94, 95,
    97
  overview, 6-7
  as peers, 6
  per-client processes, 60-67
  per-client threads, 67-70
  servers vs., 7, 12
  TCP clients, 12-17
  UDP clients, 36-39
close(), 97-99
  API reference, 117
  child and parent processes
    and, 63
  data in **SendQ** and, 99
  destroying socket instances,
    10
  graceful close, 97
  linger behavior, 99
  one application calls first, 97,
    98, 99
  return values, 10
  shutdown() vs., 97, 99
  simultaneous calls to, 97, 98
  SO_LINGER socket option, 45
  syntax, 10
  TCP client connection, 12, 13
  TCP server connection, 17,
    18
Closed state, 94
closing connections, 97-100
  close() vs. shutdown(), 97, 99
  data in **SendQ** and, 99
  graceful close, 97
  simultaneous calls to
    close(), 97, 98
  Time-Wait state and, 99-100
  using linger behavior, 99
  when one application calls
    close() first, 97, 98, 99
communication channels, 3, 5
concurrent servers, 60
connect()
  API reference, 113
  blocking, 50
  client-side connection
    establishment, 93-94
  connection time problems,
    60

nonblocking, 50, 51
opening handshake, 94
return values, 94
syntax, 12
for TCP clients, 12, 17
in TCPEchoClient.c, 15
TCPEchoServer.c and, 21
timeout of, 94
UDPEchoClient.c and, 36, 38
Connecting state, 95
connecting with TCP, 93-97
  accept() processing, 95-97
  client-side connection
    establishment, 93-94
  incoming connection request
    processing, 95, 96
  opening handshake, 94, 95,
    97
  server-side socket setup,
    94-97
constrained multitasking, 70-72
  overview, 70-71
  TCPEchoServer-ForkN.c,
    71-72
constrained-multitasking
  servers, 70
CreateTCPServerSocket(), 63
CreateTCPServerSocket.c, 65

data structures, 87-88, 111-112
datagram sockets, 7
deadlock, 91-92
delimiters of fields, 26
Delivered, 89-91, 99
demultiplexing, 100-102
deposits, 25, 26-27
DieWithError.c, 16-17
directed broadcast, 77-78
DNS (Domain Name System),
  103, 104
domain name service, 103-108
  finding service information
    by name, 106-108
  information sources, 103
  mapping between names
    and Internet addresses,
    104-106
  overview, 103
Domain Name System (DNS),
  103, 104
dotted-quad notation, 6

EADDRINUSE, 100, 101, 112
EAGAIN, 50
ECONNREFUSED, 94

EINPROGRESS, 50, 51
EINTR
  signal handling and, 49
  in UDPEchoClient-Timeout.c,
    56, 59
  in UDPEchoServer-SIGIO.c, 55
  with zombies, 64
encoding data, 26-28
  binary numbers, 27-28
  byte ordering, 28-30
  character encoding, 26
  framing, 31-33
  numbers as text strings,
    26-27, 32-33
  presentation service, 33
end-to-end transport protocols
  defined, 5
  specifying for socket
    instances, 9-10
errno, 16, 55, 59, 94, 104
Established state, 93, 96, 97
ETIMEDOUT, 94, 99
EWOULDBLOCK, 50, 51, 55, 89
exit(), 63

FASYNC, 52, 55
fcntl(), 51, 52
FD_CLR(), 73
FD_ISSET(), 73
fd_set, 73
FD_SET(), 73
FD_ZERO(), 73
F_GETFL, 51
fields of messages, 25, 26
FIFO queues, 87, 89-93
flow control, 91
fork(), 60, 61, 63
framing messages, 31-33
F_SETFL, 51
F_SETOWN, 55

gethostbyaddr(), 105, 121
gethostbyname(), 104, 105, 120,
  121
gethostname(), 105-106, 120
getpeername(), 66-67, 114-115
getpid(), 69
getservbyname(), 106-108, 121
getservbyport(), 108, 122
getsockname(), 66-67, 113
getsockopt()
  API reference, 118
  commonly used options, 45
  syntax, 43
  using, 44

graceful close, 97

HandleTCPClient(), 63
HandleTCPClient.c, 21-22
handshake (TCP)
    closing, 97-100
    opening, 94, 95, 97
Herman, Ted, 23
h_errno, 104
hostent, 104-106, 120, 121
hosts
    addresses, 6
    defined, 3
    INADDR_ANY wildcard for,
      18, 20
    names, 6
    in TCP/IP network, 4
htonl()
    API reference, 119-120
    byte order and, 29
    TCPEchoServer.c and, 20
htons()
    API reference, 119-120
    byte order and, 29
    ResolveService() and,
      108
    TCPEchoClient.c and, 15
    TCPEchoServer.c and, 20

in_addr, 15
INADDR_ANY
    bind() call and, 94-95
    ip_mreq and, 85
    SO_REUSEADDR and, 102
    TCP server wildcard, 18, 20,
      94
    in TCPEchoServer.c, 20
inet_addr(), 15, 21, 119
inet_ntoa(), 21, 119
Internet addresses
    clients and, 7
    dotted-quad notation, 6
    host names and, 6
    local, 87, 88
    mapping between names
      and, 104-106
    overview, 6
    port numbers and, 6
    remote, 87, 88
    usage in this book, 6
Internet Assigned Number
    Authority (IANA), 7
Internet Protocol. *See* IP (Internet
    Protocol)
InterruptSignalHandler(), 49

IP addresses. *See* Internet
    addresses
IP (Internet Protocol)
    IPv6, 6, 104
    TCP/IP implementation, 4-5
IP_ADD_MEMBERSHIP, 85
ip_mreq, 84-85
IPPROTO_IP socket options, 45
IPPROTO_TCP
    socket options, 44, 45
    as socket() parameter, 9, 112
    TCP client connection, 12
IPPROTO_UDP
    as socket() parameter, 9, 112
    in UDPEchoClient.c, 38
    in UDPEchoServer.c, 41
iterative servers, 60

joining a multicast group, 83

kill, 49

Layers of TCP/IP, 4-5
least-significant byte, 29
life cycle of TCP sockets, 93-100
    closing a connection, 97-100
    connecting, 93-97
linger, 99
listen()
    API reference, 114
    return values, 18
    server call to, 93, 95
    syntax, 18
    TCP server connection, 17,
      18
    in TCPEchoServer.c, 21
    UDPEchoServer.c and, 41
Little-Endian architecture, 28-29
local broadcast, 77
local Internet addresses, 87, 88

mapping between names and
    Internet addresses,
    104-106
maximally aligned data, 31
memset(), 15
message construction, 25-33
    alignment, 30-31
    byte ordering, 28-30
    encoding data, 26-28
    fields, 25
    framing, 31-33
    padding bytes, 30-31
    parsing, 31-33

UDP and message
    boundaries, 36, 41
most-significant byte, 28
MSG_DONTWAIT, 51
MSG_PEEK, 41, 42
msgStruct, 28-29, 30
MSG_WAITALL, 93
multicast, 81-85
    broadcast vs., 85
    described, 77
    multicast group, 83
    receiver, 83-85
    sender, 81-83
    unicast vs., 81
multicast group, 83
MulticastReceiver.c, 83-85
MulticastSender.c, 81-83
multiple recipients, 77-85
    broadcast, 77-81
    broadcast vs. multicast, 85
    multicast, 77, 81-85
    unicast, *77*
multiplexing, 72-77
    demultiplexing, 100-102
    need for, 72
    select(), 72-74, 76-77
    TCPEchoServer-Select.c,
      74-77
multitasking, 60-72
    concurrent servers, 60
    constrained, 70-72
    iterative server problems
      and, 60
    per-client processes, 60-67
    per-client threads, 67-70

name service. *See* domain name
    service
names
    finding service information
      by name, 106-108
    for hosts, 6
    mapping between names
      and Internet addresses,
      104-106
network byte order, 29-30
Network File System (NFS), 33
network layer, 5
networks
    overview, 3-5
    TCP/IP networks, 4-5
NFS (Network File System), 33
nonblocking I/O, 50-59
    asynchronous I/O, 51-55
    need for, 50

nonblocking I/O *(continued)*
  nonblocking sockets, 50–51
  timeouts, 56–59
ntohl(), 29, 119–120
ntohs(), 29, 119–120

O_ASYNC, 55
O_NONBLOCK, 51, 55
open(), 10

packets
  defined, 4
  IP address in, 5
  matching to sockets, 100–102
padding bytes, 30–31
parent processes, 60, 63–64, 72
parsing messages, 31–33
pause(), 48
peer, 6
pending signals, 49
per-client processes, 60–67
  AcceptTCPConnection.c, 66
  child processes, 60, 63, 64
  constrained multitasking,
    70–72
  CreateTCPServerSocket.c, 65
  overhead from, 67, 70
  overview, 60–61
  parent processes, 60, 63–64
  per-client threads vs., 69–70
  phases in connection setup,
    61
  TCPEchoServer-Fork.c, 60–64
  TCPEchoServer.h, 61, 64–65
  zombies, 60, 64
per-client threads, 67–70
  constrained multitasking,
    70–71
  overhead from, 70
  per-client processes vs.,
    69–70
  performance advantages, 67
  TCPEchoServer-Thread.c,
    67–69
performance issues
  buffering, 92–93
  constrained-multitasking
    servers, 70
  per-client processes, 67, 70
  per-client threads, 67, 70
  throughput, 92–93
PF_INET
  AF_INET vs., 11
  end-to-end protocols, 9, 112
  TCP client connection, 12

port numbers
  assignment, 7
  binding to servers, 17–18
  demultiplexing, 100–102
  local, 87, 88
  overview, 5, 6
  remote, 87, 88
  as socket identifier, 8
presentation service, 33
printf(), 16, 59
process ID, 63
processes. *See* per-client
    processes
protocol family, 4, 9
protocols. *See also specific*
    protocols
  application protocols, 25
  defined, 4
pthread_create(), 69
pthread_detach(), 69
pthread_self(), 69

ReceiveMessage(), 32–33
recv(), 89–93
  API reference, 116
  blocking, 50
  buffering in TCP and, 89–91
  closed connection and, 99
  data structures and, 88
  deadlock, 91–92
  default behavior, 13
  Established state and, 93
  framing and, 31, 32, 33
  HandleTCPClient.c and, 21
  multiple I/O channels and,
    72
  nonblocking, 51
  performance issues, 92–93
  recvfrom() vs., 35, 41–42
  select() for timeout
    implementation, 77
  send() lack of
    correspondence, 89–91
  send() semantics and, 115
  SO_RCVLOWAT socket option,
    45
  syntax, 12
  TCP client connection, 12–13
  TCP server connection, 17,
    18
  in TCPEchoClient.c, 16
  in UDPEchoServer.c, 41
recvfrom()
  API reference, 116–117
  blocking, 50

buffer size for, 42
  data structures and, 88
  MSG_PEEK with, 41, 42
  nonblocking, 51
  recv() vs., 35, 41–42
  syntax, 35
  timeouts, 56
  in UDPEchoClient.c, 38, 39
  in UDPEchoClient-Timeout.c,
    59
  in UDPEchoServer.c, 41
  in UDPEchoServer-SIGIO.c, 52,
    55
RecvQ, 89–92, 97, 99
reliable byte-stream channel, 5
remote Internet addresses, 87,
    88
Remote Procedure Call (RPC), 33
ResolveName(), 104–105, 106
ResolveService(), 106–108
routers, 3–4
RPC (Remote Procedure Call), 33

sa_flags, 47, 64
SA_NOCLDWAIT, 64
SA_NODEFER, 47
SA_RESTART, 64
select(), 72–74
  connection completion and,
    51
  descriptor lists monitored
    by, 73
  NULL descriptor vectors, 73
  syntax, 73
  system-provided macros, 73
  in TCPEchoServer-Select.c,
    76–77
send(), 89–93
  API reference, 115
  blocking, 50
  buffering in TCP and, 89–91
  data structures and, 88
  deadlock, 91–92
  default behavior, 12–13
  effective size of call to, 93
  Established state and, 93
  integers with, 28
  nonblocking, 51
  performance issues, 92–93
  recv() lack of
    correspondence, 89–91
  recv() syntax and, 116
  sendto() vs., 35, 41
  with sprintf(), 26–27
  syntax, 12

TCP client connection, 12-13
TCP server connection, 17, 18
    in TCPEchoClient.c, 16
SendQ, 89-93, 97, 99
sendto()
    API reference, 115-116
    data structures and, 88
    nonblocking, 51
    parameters, 35
    send() vs., 35, 41
    syntax, 35
    in UDPEchoClient.c, 38
    in UDPEchoServer.c, 41
    in UDPEchoServer-SIGIO.c, 55
servent, 106, 108, 121, 122
servers
    accept() processing, 95-97
    clients vs., 7, 12
    closing handshake, 97-100
    concurrent, 60
    constrained-multitasking, 70
    incoming connection request
        processing, 95, 96
    iterative, 60
    opening handshake, 94, 95, 97
    overview, 6-7
    as peers, 6
    server-side socket setup, 94-96
    TCP servers, 17-22
    UDP servers, 39-41
setsockopt()
    API reference, 118
    commonly used options, 45
    linger with, 99
    syntax, 43
    using, 44
shutdown()
    API reference, 117
    close() vs., 97, 99
    data in **SendQ** and, 99
    graceful close, 97
    syntax, 99
SHUT_WR, 99
sigaction, 46, 55, 64
sigaction()
    asynchronous I/O, 52
    example, 47-49
    interrupted system calls and, 64
    return values, 46
    sa_flags field, 47
    sa_handler field, 47

sa_mask field, 47
    syntax, 46
SigAction.c, 47-49
    described, 47
    explanation, 48-49
    listing, 48
sigaddset(), 47
SIGALRM
    default behavior, 46
    timeouts, 56
    triggering event, 46
    in UDPEchoClient-Timeout.c, 56, 59
SIGCHLD, 46, 64
sigdelset(), 47
SIG_DFL, 47
sigemptyset(), 47
sigfillset(), 47
SIG_IGN, 47
SIGINT, 46, 47, 49
SIGIO
    asynchronous I/O, 52, 55
    default behavior, 46
    SIGALRM and, 56
    triggering event, 46
    UDPEchoServer-SIGIO.c, 52-55
SIGIOHandler(), 54-55
signals, 44-50
    blocking and, 49
    default behavior, 46
    described, 44
    pending, 49
    possible responses to, 44, 46
    triggering events, 46
SIGPIPE, 46, 49-50
sigset_t, 47
SIGTERM, 49
Simple Network Management
    Protocol (SNMP), 33
size aligned data, 30-31
sleep(), 60
SNMP (Simple Network
    Management Protocol), 33
SO_BROADCAST, 79
sockaddr
    accept() and, 114
    API reference, 111
    bind() and, 112
    byte order and, 29-30
    connect() and, 113
    getpeername() and, 66, 67, 114-115
    getsockname() and, 113
    overview, 10-11

recvfrom() and, 117
    sendto() and, 116
    sockaddr_in vs., 11
    TCP client connection, 12
    TCP server setup, 17, 18
    TCPEchoClient.c and, 15
sockaddr_in, 112
    accept() and, 114
    API reference, 111-112
    getpeername() and, 67
    overview, 11
    sockaddr vs., 11
    TCP client connection, 12
    TCP server setup, 18
    in TCPEchoClient.c, 15
    in TCPEchoServer.c, 20, 21
SOCK_DGRAM
    as socket() parameter, 9, 112
    in UDPEchoClient.c, 38
    in UDPEchoServer.c, 41
socket(), 9-12
    address specification, 10-11
    API reference, 112
    bind() and, 112
    connect() and, 113
    creating socket instances, 9-10
    data structures and, 87
    getpeername() and, 115
    getsockname() and, 113
    listen() and, 114
    return values, 10
    socket options and, 43
    syntax, 9-10
    TCP client connection, 12
    TCP server setup, 17, 18
socket descriptor, 8, 10, 12, 18, 87
socket options, 43-44, 45
socket programming
    multiple recipients, 77-85
    multiplexing, 72-77
    multitasking, 60-72
    nonblocking I/O, 50-59
    signals, 44, 46-50
    socket options, 43-44, 45
sockets
    addresses of, 8, 10-11
    creating instances, 9-10
    datagram, 7
    destroying instances, 10
    life cycle, 93-100
    matching packets to, 100-102
    nonblocking, 50-51

sockets *(continued)*
  overview, 7-8
  stream, 7
SOCK_STREAM
  as socket() parameter, 9, 112
  TCP client connection, 12
SO_LINGER, 99
SOL_SOCKET level options, 44,
    45
SO_RCVBUF, 91, 93
SO_REUSEADDR, 102, 112
SO_SNDBUF, 91, 93
sprintf(), 26-27
stream sockets, 7
struct MsgBuf variable, 32

TCP (Transmission Control
    Protocol)
  buffering and, 89-93
  data structures, 87-88
  overview, 5
  stream sockets, 7
  TCP/IP implementation, 4-5
TCP/IP, 4-5
TCPEchoClient.c, 13-17
  communication with echo
    server, 17
  described, 13
  error function, 16-17
  explanation, 15-16
  listing, 13-15
  ResolveName() in, 105
  ResolveService() in, 107
TCPEchoServer.c, 19-22
  described, 19
  explanation, 20-22
  HandleTCPClient(), 21-22
  listing, 19-20
  outputs, 22
  thought questions, 23
TCPEchoServer-Fork.c, 60-64
TCPEchoServer.h, 61, 64-65
  AcceptTCPConnection.c, 66

CreateTCPServerSocket.c, 65
  described, 60-61
  explanation, 63-64
  listing, 61-62
  TCPEchoServer.h, 61, 64-65
TCPEchoServer-ForkN.c, 71-72
TCPEchoServer-Select.c, 74-77
  described, 74
  explanation, 76-77
  listing, 74-76
TCPEchoServer-Thread.c, 67-69
  described, 67
  explanation, 68-69
  listing, 67-68
text strings
  binary/string conversion,
    119-120
  numbers as, 26-27, 32-33
ThreadArgs, 69
ThreadMain(), 69
threads, 67, 69-70. *See also*
    per-client threads
three-way handshake. *See*
    handshake (TCP)
throughput, 92-93
Time-Wait state, 99-100
timeouts, 56-59
  of handshake, 94
  overview, 56
  UDPEchoClient-Timeout.c,
    56-59
timeval, 74
Transmission Control Protocol.
    See TCP (Transmission
    Control Protocol)
transport layer, 5

UDP sockets, 35-42
  matching packets to,
    100-101
  message boundaries and, 36,
    41
  receiving routine, 35-36

sending routine, 35
  TCP sockets vs., 35, 36, 41
  UDP clients, 36-39
  UDP servers, 39-41
UDP (User Datagram Protocol),
    5, 7
UDPEchoClient.c, 36-39
  described, 36
  explanation, 38-39
  listing, 36-38
  lost UDP datagrams and, 50
UDPEchoClient-Timeout.c, 56-59
  described, 56
  explanation, 59
  listing, 56-59
UDPEchoServer.c, 39-41
  described, 39
  explanation, 41
  listing, 39-40
UDPEchoServer-SIGIO.c, 52-55
  described, 52
  explanation, 54-55
  listing, 52-54
unicast, 77, 81
Universal Resource Locators
    (URLs), 7
UNIX
  multitasking, 60
  signals, 46
  zombie handling in, 64
URLs (Universal Resource
    Locators), 7
UseIdleTime(), 54, 55
User Datagram Protocol (UDP),
    5, 7

waitpid(), 60, 64
white space, 26
withdrawals, 25, 26-27
WNOHANG, 64

zombies, 60, 64